The Lemurian Revival

(The Key to Success in Life and Leadership)

The Lemurian Revival

(The Key to Success in Life and Leadership)

R. Sivadas

Email: rsivadas@gmail.com
Website: www.thelemurianrevival.com, www.pragyanconsult.com
LinkedIn: http://linkedin.com/in/rsivadas
January 2021

The Lemurian Revival

(The Key to Success in Life and Leadership)

ISBN: 978-81-946019-1-3

E-ISBN: 978-81-946019-2-0

Typeset and Cover designed by Chennai Publishing Services Pvt. Ltd., Chennai, India

Author's Note

There is an old, persistent Tamil tradition about a land that existed south of India called Kumari Kandam (continent), a belief that is linked to the myth of the lost land of Lemuria, a figment of Western imagination. Accounts of the lost continent vary, but the common theme is that a large area went under the ocean as a result of geological cataclysms, a theory that geologists of today do not subscribe to.

At the peak of it's civilization, the Lemurian people are supposed to have been both highly evolved and very spiritual.

According to legend, the Prophets & Avatars of Lemuria also knew that when the new time came, after the flood, mankind would move away from the sacred teachings. The prophets knew that there would be a very long period of time (about 13,000 to 26,000 years) during which the teachings would have to be kept hidden. They knew that one day that cycle would end and the teachings would once again emerge from each and every person – that time being now...

This book explores some of these teachings that can help you achieve inner alchemy and operate from a place of peace and contentment. This book seeks to revive and activate the memory of the mythological Lemuria in each of you, it will not necessarily take the form of information. Instead, it will simply take the form of your own growth and inner wisdom and peace.

Preface

Let me begin with a story that captures the essence of this book – building inner resilience in the face of the most trying of circumstances, overcoming physical obstacles and emotional fears, and coming out victorious.

> Michael Phelps, one of the greatest Olympian swimmers of all time, has a record-breaking 28 Olympic medals overall of which 23 are gold. This is more than the Olympic medals tally that many countries have overall across all sports. However, none of it came easy. Phelps said that he trained every day of the week because in his own words, "in swimming, if you miss one day, it takes two days to get back. I spent six years straight not missing a single day of training. I was getting so much more benefit out of that than other athletes who were swimming for 6 days. I hate losing more than I love winning." It was the determination of not letting anything come in the way of him achieving his dream. Passion, hard work, mental toughness, and agility sum up his success formula.
>
> Few know that as a child he suffered from attention-deficit hyperactivity disorder (ADHD) and was on medication for quite some time. People with ADHD suffer from restlessness, impulsiveness, and a very short attention span. However, they also have an incredible capacity to remain focused on an activity they are passionate about. Phelps used this trait to achieve success by channelling his energy and focus and was able to exploit the positive side of ADHD.
>
> Phelps beat the most disciplined and strongest swimmers in the world and he is an inspiring example to anyone who suffers from a mental disorder or any other physical disability. Visualization is another technique that he used before every swim and he started this at the age of 7. He has proved that there are no limits to success once one is passionate about what he is doing and works hard with focus to achieve his/her objective with a disciplined mind and controlled emotions. In the process he also developed as a person and post retirement he works as a mental health advocate working on a problem that he had himself faced and one he was familiar with.

This is the theme that I propose to build in this book and will show step by step how to meet failures and setbacks and build resilience. It all starts and ends with the mind. But a better appreciation of why one must follow some practices and how research supports a practice will be explored as we go along.

In my previous book, *Failure to Millionaire: How I Created a Successful Company and How You Can Too!*, in which I outlined my entrepreneurial journey, I had stressed that failures are a key to success. I had elaborated on the many failures that I had to go through to taste a couple of successes. The incident of the promoter of Café Coffee Day committing suicide while regrettable and tragic also underlines the pressures and priorities that an entrepreneur and manager goes through. It is not just in the world of business, but also pervades almost all areas of life where uncertainty and the consequent stress is the new norm. Especially so with teens who today encounter enormous stress arising from social, psychological, and societal pressures that includes

(i) Mental illness/depression
(ii) Peer pressure and the need to be accepted in a group
(iii) Academic pressure

(iv) Uncertainty about the future
(v) Parental pressure
(vi) Rapid changes in technology.

Businessmen, entrepreneurs, managers, professionals, youngsters, and students all need to develop the resilience to deal with these pressures and that calls for developing inner strength. It is my firm conviction that the skills required for any task can be acquired (in any case they keep changing and therefore it needs to be learnt and relearnt) but the inner resilience and strength will define the difference between success and failure. This inner resilience will also help one lead a happy life.

Failures are a part and parcel of life. Through all of these failures, the ability of an individual to withstand the stresses and strains of repeated failures, learn from them, and move on is a skill that is often underrated and unrecognized.

One can develop the ability to bounce back from difficult situations by cultivating these four traits as a leader:

1. Resilience, which depends a great deal on one's self-confidence and which means a firm and expanded mind.
2. Flexibility, which requires a strong purpose and self-discipline along with a flexible/adaptable mind.
3. Compassion, which calls for a soft mind.
4. Perspective, which means a bird's eye view of situations and people.

During my own journey, I realized that apart from all the other skills and external processes and systems, to be successful one must also have the ability to manage oneself and keep fit physically, physiologically, mentally, and spiritually. My response to some of these stresses was to combine work with a journey of self-discovery that over a period of 30 years took me to many Himalayan masters, Buddhist monks, and religious scholars. I learnt, observed, and practised several meditation practices. I am convinced that the new paradigm of leadership begins with managing oneself. One needs to look inwards and understand what is happening internally and learn to manage one's own emotions and thought processes, among them all the negative and base thought processes and resultant emotions of desires, anger, greed, jealousy, etc. Along the way, it became clear to me that tremendous wisdom lies in these teachings and these are as relevant if not more relevant today than ever before. Shorn of its religious connotations and rituals, many of these practices could be adapted to organizations and individuals to ensure increase in productivity, resilience, and stability amongst employees as also to increase the emotional and spiritual quotient of entrepreneurs, managers, students, and employees. I believe that the spiritual quotient is as important, faced as we are, with the declining standards in values and ethics among corporate executives as also the increasing moral dilemma that managers face today. The ongoing Covid-19 epidemic underscores the importance of resilience and managing the self, given the drastic changes that it has brought to our day-to-day lives. Unfortunately, isolation from society, the inflow of bleak coronavirus-related information, the fear of contracting Covid-19, the looming economic recession, and a sense of helplessness are all impacting people's mental well-being adversely, causing a lot of stress, anxiety, depression, and other mental health concerns. A survey by the Indian Psychiatric Society revealed that during Lockdown 1.0 itself, there had been an alarming 20% rise in mental health concerns. The crisis has also compounded the issues of those with existing psychological symptoms.

The effect of this crisis has been devastating on the economy as well. According to the Centre for Monitoring Indian Economy (CMEI):

- The average employment in India reduced from 404 million in March 2019 to 282 million in April 2020, which means that about 122 million people have lost their jobs, including 27 million youth.
- From an estimated 78 million entrepreneurs and businesses in 2019–2020, India was down to approximately 60 million by April 2020.
- Apart from job losses, the physical and emotional burdens of stress and anxiety from this uncertainty also affect people's job performance and ultimately has an impact on job loyalty, making this a critical issue for employers to focus on.

In addition, the stresses and rigors of the current ultra-competitive marketplace, with change being the only constant, takes a heavy toll on managers and employees who are finding it increasingly difficult to balance their lives. Spirituality (as distinct from religion) helps gives that sense of balance and direction to one's life and keeps it interesting and refreshing. It is in this context that Inner Mastery has become so important. I did a quick survey of more than 150 working professionals aged between 30 and 50 years in India over 3 months of Covid-19 lockdown. The survey revealed that approximately 40% chose some form of yoga/meditation to manage stress. It also indicated that 28% said that they watched TV/movies/serials to keep their minds occupied and 20% chose to smoke or drink or use other forms of socializing to divert their attention. Twelve per cent were ambivalent and said that they tried multiple things. The fact that nearly 40% of those talked to indicated recourse to yoga/meditation shows the importance of building inner resilience and mental strength in meeting adversity.

Mindfulness is one such technique that has become quite popular in the West, mainly taken from Buddhist practices. While mindfulness has been researched quiet extensively in the West both from an impact perspective and from a process perspective, I believe that the practice itself could be extended, expanded, and made more effective. It is not as easy as it is made out to be and to have a lasting impact one needs to understand the foundations of mindfulness/awareness/meditation practices and strengthen the foundations of the practice by understanding oneself better.

I have therefore thought it necessary to delve a little into detail of what we as human beings are comprised of (something that we rarely pause to think). This I have done from a Tantric and Vedantic (Upanishadic) perspective. Upanishads are Indian Vedic scriptures that are purely philosophical in nature and go beyond rituals and religion and which are normally found at the end portion of the Vedas. These go beyond religion and are the fountainhead of pure spirituality based on an enquiry within. To that extent, it helps us in realizing management guru Peter Drucker's vision of meeting the existential challenge that he enumerated: "The society of organizations forces the individual to ask of himself: 'Who am I?' 'What do I want to be?' 'What do I want to put into life and what do I want to get out of it?'".

There is nothing religious about these insights which are based on deep contemplation and an inward journey and have withstood the passage of time. I have tried to put these insights in a way that it is useful for practice in a corporate context. I do not claim any originality in this work except as I have said to put it in a non-religious, non-cultural context shorn of associated terminology that may not make sense to a layperson. I have also tried to support these conclusions with modern scientific research wherever available. I believe that a better and simplified understanding of our persona going beyond the superficial will help put our lives back in context and give it better meaning and purpose as Drucker so eloquently put it so many years back.

This will also hopefully help make managers and entrepreneurs manage from the heart as against a purely materialistic view of the world; people who have the greater good of the society at the heart of all their actions and who are not bound by selfishness and a consciousness that is restricted only to the promotion of their own self-interests. Education finally must also instil some values and societal concerns as so well-articulated by someone who saw the horrors of brilliant minds gone astray.

> I am a survivor of a concentration camp. My eyes saw what no person should witness: gas chambers built by learned engineers, Children poisoned educated physicians. Infants killed by trained nurses. Women and babies shot by high school and college graduates. So, I am suspicious of education.

My request is, Help your children become human. Your efforts must never produce learned monsters or skilled psychopaths. Reading, writing, and arithmetic are important only if they serve to make children more human.

Dr. Haim Ginott
Child Psychologist and Holocaust Survivor

In my opinion, this will also enable the mindfulness practice to be expanded since the body and mind are so interconnected and so is the connection to the larger whole – the cosmos. A better understanding of consciousness (an Eastern perspective) of matter and energy (which was expounded thousands of years back in the Upanishads and which is currently being confirmed by science), and the way our lives are intertwined will help us to deal with our minds, bodies, intellect, and awareness in an expanded and wholistic way. The world is moving towards an expanded consciousness. This will no doubt have a positive impact on society as a whole as more and more people adopt this as a way of life and deal with personal and societal issues in a way that is so aptly mentioned in the Upanishads as "May All become Happy, May All be Free from Illness, May All See what is Auspicious, May no one Suffer, Peace, Peace, Peace."

This book integrates the following sources of insight on mastering one's inner environment:

- Recent scientific advances (from psychology, neuroscience, sociology, and cognitive-behaviour therapy)
- Case studies of the inner lives of great achievers (such as Lincoln, Gandhi, Dalai Lama, Vivekananda, Nelson Mandela, Bill Gates, and Steve Jobs)
- Lessons from great spiritual masters.

This book is structured in such a way that it interweaves the research results from modern scientific research with some timeless principles from ancient practices and relevant stories that explain the concepts in a simple easily understood fashion in such a way that the reader gets a perspective of why he should be doing some of the recommended practices and some of the benefits that accrue with scientific proof wherever available.

Chapter 1 lays the foundation of the social and business environment currently and the importance of emotional resilience in a post Covid-19 world. While we have emphasized the knowledge worker, this is applicable to virtually everyone as we live in a knowledge world driven by digital technology which is put to use in varying degrees by almost everyone whether for personal or official use. Chapter 2 examines some enduring leadership principles based on the lives of some of the acknowledged great leaders who have impacted many lives. These leadership principles are then classified into four main buckets that form the basis of our discussions and analysis as we move forward. These leadership principles are as applicable to all whether a student, a housewife, an entrepreneur, a businessman, an executive, a politician, etc.

Chapter 3 then develops on the theme of these leadership principles as it relates to one's mind and emotions. To understand how to control one's mind and emotions, one needs to understand what we are comprised of and what the mind actually is. It therefore looks at the constituents of the self in great detail. Chapter 4 follows this through with a more in-depth understanding of what constitutes the mind. The mind is broken up into its constituent parts, which facilitates better understanding and action. It is normally understood that the mind is located in the brain and without the brain the mind does not function. These chapters will help one in understanding who he/she is and what is his/her true self? Some of the issues explored are the following:

One is not just his/her physical body. What exactly is the mind? How is the mind related to one's emotions? How is one's mind and breath related? How can one control his/her mind by controlling the breath and using breath as the gateway to his/her mind. Understanding oneself better and building self-confidence from within.

Chapter 5 looks at what constitutes the brain and what are its constituent parts and its function. Chapter 6 then looks at the neurosciences behind the functioning of the brain and the takeaways from the current scientific research. Chapter 7 expands on this theme and looks at how neuroplasticity of the brain is perhaps something that we can leverage for immense benefit which is enumerated and which can be done through meditation. These chapters help in understanding issues such as the benefits of meditation from a scientific perspective, erasing one's mental stereotypes and redefining his/her identity based on meditation practices.

Meditation is a very important tool in the arsenal of a leader and can be effectively used to train and calm the mind. This is dealt in detail in Chapter 8. While meditation and mindfulness (mindfulness practices are one tool used to meditate) are very important, they are far more effective if one learns to focus the mind for which concentration practices are a very important tool. Chapter 9 explains concentration in detail along with suggesting some exercises that help one to concentrate better. Chapter 10 talks about physical postures and breath control as a prelude to concentration as without physical health concentration is extremely difficult. Besides it is easier to control the mind through the breath than directly. This is dealt with in detail in this chapter. Chapter 11 looks at some practices that have not been explored/validated as yet by any current scientific research but has been in vogue with great results for centuries in yogic practice. Chapter 12 then brings all the individual parts into a comprehensive 4D practice which is what we had analysed as important attributes for life and leadership in Chapter 2. These chapters help in discovering one's purposes and aligning them with the values one hold dear while helping to define action plans. Also explained are some powerful and latest scientific findings on the pursuit of happiness.

Mindfulness and heartfulness are the themes talked about in Chapter 13 as they are widely practised especially in the West and are a very useful meditation tools. However, it can be made far more effective with some of the practices/exercises that have been suggested in the appendices. No meditation is as effective as the one that brings in our positive emotions into play (also described as heartfulness meditation) and therefore Chapter 13 talks about visualization techniques that help to develop qualities of the heart such as compassion, gratitude, kindness, empathy, love, and so on. The final chapter (Chapter 14) provides a summary of the entire book and its potential impact on a person who follows some of these practices. Interweaved through the book are scientific research and practices on the following:

- *Mastering the intellect*. Understanding one's intellect and the emotional mind. Ways to build a strong intellect and use of logical reasoning. Latest research and findings in psychology on the use of logic.
- *Mastering emotions*. Understanding one's emotions and the latest scientific findings on the costs and benefits of key emotions: anger, greed, jealousy, fear, anxiety, and optimism. Making emotions work for one. Using visualization meditations to change beliefs, thoughts, and emotions.
- *Managing for results*. Cultivating self-discipline and the latest scientific findings on how self-discipline shapes one's success in life and leadership. Learning how one's thoughts and imagination affect one's performance. Using affirmations and visualization to boost one's performance.
- *Dispassion*. Self-enquiry and self-control. How to succeed by focusing on the task and not the result – the principle of nonattachment. Limitations to operating at full potential. How one's body produces energy and energy leakages. How to recharge one's energy with his/her breath and his/her thoughts (backed by science). Manage one's health and diet.

Foreword

Of all the people who I know personally, Sivadas Raghava is uniquely qualified to write a book on success in life and leadership, and how that can be linked to spiritual growth and inner wisdom. After his MBA from the prestigious IIM, Ahmedabad, he has had stellar success in his professional career and went on to achieve great heights as an entrepreneur in the knowledge economy. He has also had a very fulfilling family life. While doing total justice to these different realms, over the last few decades, he had also simultaneously turned his attention to his inner world, which many in our contemporary world ignore until it is too late in life. In this domain of the spiritual world too, he has achieved great heights. In a nutshell, his life epitomizes pursuit of the four cornerstones of Indian philosophy: Dharma (righteousness), Artha (achieving material prosperity), Kaama (entertainment, enjoyment, and pleasures), and Moksha (liberation from the relentless cycles of birth and death and from the bondage of Samsara). This journey is indeed enviable and could be a role model for many who aspire to walk the path he has pursued.

In his book, *The Lemurian Revival*, the author has deeply explored the inner world and showcased the salubrious impact that such a journey would have to enrich our lives, if only we choose the path that he points to. He is an active practitioner and strong advocate of yoga and meditation for all-round personal growth. Sivadas is an avid trekker and badminton player. Personally, he is an embodiment of the principle "a strong body houses a strong mind," which is key to clarity of thought and spiritual awakening. He is a serial entrepreneur and business leader with strengths in entrepreneurship and innovation, Sivadas has successfully completed three rounds of exits in knowledge-based entrepreneurial ventures. So, I was excited to read what he had to offer as a talisman to good leadership and life, through his path-breaking book.

I am impressed by his vast knowledge about mythology, spirituality, and the role these play in shaping values that are at the core of oneself. He has the unique ability to link these deep personal values for extrapolating them to aspects of effective leadership and for using them to help us lead a meaningful life.

This book explores some of the many ancient eastern teachings that can help one achieve inner calm and operate from a platform of peace and contentment. It seeks to revive and activate the memory of the mythological Lemuria in each reader. Lemuria was a mythological continent in southern India which disappeared under the oceans – where the inhabitants were supposed to be highly evolved and very spiritual. This book serves as a guide for each reader to help one find his/her own Lemuria. It is truly a process of self-discovery.

This book draws upon the learnings from the Upanishads – Indian Vedic scriptures that are purely philosophical in nature and go beyond rituals and religion. The Upanishads are believed to be the earliest texts known to humanity, which discuss spirituality based on introspection and internal enquiry. In his book, Sivadas has aptly captured this spirit of one's internal journey:

> To that extent, it (the Upanishads) helps us in realizing management guru Peter Drucker's vision of meeting the existential challenge that he enumerated: "The society of organizations forces the individual to ask of himself: 'Who am I?' 'What do I want to be?' 'What do I want to put into life?' and 'What do I want to get out of it?'"

A better understanding of consciousness and the way our lives are intertwined will help us deal with our minds, bodies, and awareness in a holistic way. The world is moving towards an expanded consciousness. Consciousness and mindfulness are deeply interrelated. Having more and more people thinking and acting consciously and adopting this way of life will have a positive impact on society. As noted by Sivadas, this is aptly captured in the Upanishads: "May All become Happy, May All be Free from Illness, May All See what is auspicious, May No One Suffer, Peace, Peace, Peace."

This book is structured in a way that it interweaves the results of modern scientific research from psychology, neuroscience, sociology, and cognitive-behaviour therapy with some timeless principles of ancient practices and relevant stories of the inner lives of great achievers (such as Abraham Lincoln, Mahatma Gandhi, The Dalai Lama, Swami Vivekananda, Nelson Mandela, Bill Gates, and Steve Jobs). The concepts are laid out in a simple, easily understood manner, in such a way that the reader gets a perspective of why she/he should be following some of the recommended practices encapsulated in this book. It enlightens her/him of some of the benefits that accrue with diligent practice of the recommendations that Sivadas has presented to us. In this book, there is considerable emphasis on the role of mindful meditation in harnessing neuroplasticity, which is essential to achieve superior results in life, in our chosen domains.

Unique in this book is "The 4D Practice" recommended by Sivadas to get greater mastery over the mind by channelizing it from an emotional one to a more alert, aware, in-control, and focused state by practising the four D's: discrimination, dispassion or detachment, discipline, and deep desire.

The appendices offer a step-by-step guide to inner transformation. It begins with a recommendation of 25 minutes of physical exercise per day for everyone, followed by a simple and effective guide to kriya pranayama (breathing techniques). Finally, a meditation routine is laid out for daily practice. Mindful meditation is effective only if one has good physical health and follows proper breathing techniques. Meditation leads to spiritual growth, a better understanding of oneself, and ultimately mind control. It leads to enhanced concentration and mindful actions in day-to-day life. It helps cultivate both, mindfulness and heartfulness. Every journey begins with a single step and the first step towards the transformation of discovering one's internal Lemuria begins with exercise – key to a healthy body.

I am in complete agreement with the author's viewpoint that modern education does not focus enough on how to train one's mind. Neither does it teach concentration. As a result, most people struggle to concentrate on issues and problems that they encounter in life. The problem of lack of concentration gets worse with age, as worries and stress levels increase. The mind becomes even more dissipated and further loses concentration and focus. This can result in loss of mental ability and erroneous decisions – things that can negatively impact both, one's leadership style and life. This book offers solutions to break out of the negative cycle of lack of concentration.

I particularly loved Sivadas's viewpoint on meditation versus concentration. He offers a powerful insight – "Concentration can be taught using various techniques, but meditation happens." In other words, one cannot force him/herself to meditate, he/she can only practise concentration. If one does it often enough and in the right manner, meditation will ensue. Perhaps, meditation is akin to happiness. If one goes looking for it, he/she is unlikely to find it. But, if one does some things right, both meditation and happiness will come to him/her. This book is a wonderful "go to" ready reckoner for enhancing the quality of one's life, rather than run blindly behind the quantity of life, that most people blindly pursue.

In conclusion, *The Lemurian Revival* promises to be an interesting read for all those who are looking to enrich their lives and want to adopt values-based sustainable management practices. It is meant for the seeking mind that desires fulfilment both in life and in leadership!

Happy Reading!

Dr. D.V.R. Seshadri
Clinical Full Professor of Marketing and Director,
Centre for Marketing Innovation,
Indian School of Business, Gachibowli, Hyderabad.
December 1, 2020

Review

The myth of the lemurian land on one side and the current global pandemic on the other – mindfulness and heartfulness on one side and insights from neurosciences on the other side. This in many ways to me characterizes Sivadas's book.

Not a study in contrasts so to speak but a synthesis of seemingly diverse ideas to bring to the reader a bouquet of rich insights, especially for the present period.

Sivadas has gleaned insights from diverse fields to share with his readers one central message – how to live a life of meaning and happiness.

The truth is that this subject of meaning and happiness has a spiritual dimension as well as scientific dimension and both of great relevance. Sivadas does not profess to choose one over the other but merely offers to the readers an entire range of ideas. In that sense, this book is truly eclectic in its treatment and content. It is for the readers to pick and choose what they wish to explore and how much.

For many who are seeking solutions to their several challenges of living and working, it can be a hard task to figure out where to start. There are many sources of insights and information and that can often be baffling. Sivadas has done readers the great service of relying on his rich first-hand experience to curate a collection of resources which are easy to understand and put to use.

Some important aspects covered by this book are worth mentioning:

- Understanding oneself at a deeper level from a consciousness plane
- The mind and its control
- The brain and neurosciences
- The 4D practice (discrimination, dispassion, discipline, and desire)
- Meditation, mindfulness, and heartfulness
- Implications for leadership.

In many ways, meditation and mindfulness appears to be the thread that runs through the entire book.

For some, this book may appear at first glance as somewhat assorted in its scope and coverage. However, reading and reflection will lead us to recognize that this book is borne out of the author's personal experiences as well as the author's ability to synthesize from diverse fields and distil the truth and to that extent it can become distilled wisdom.

As the subtitle says, *The Lemurian Revival* attempts to offer one the key to success in life and leadership.

Happy Reading!

Ganesh Chella
Author, Consultant, and Coach
Co-Founder and Managing Director,
CFI, Founder, Totus Consulting

Acknowledgements

This book would not have happened without the spiritual spark that was lit in me by my earthly mother Smt. Leela Menon and sustained by the grace of the Divine Mother. I have a deep sense of gratefulness to both.

I thank my wife Vinitha and my children, Pranav and Ananya, for motivating me to write this book.

I thank my Guru, Avadhoot Baba Shivananda, for the inner transformation that he brought in me, ever since I met him in 2004. He taught me the way to combine spirituality with an active worldly life. He brought to life and experience the verse in the *Bhagavad Gita*: "You have the right only to action, let not your actions be guided by the desire for the fruits of that action."

My heartfelt thanks to Swami Paramarthananda whose discourses on the Upanishads, the *Bhagavad Gita*, and *Tattva Bodha* have been a source of great learning and joy. My sincere thanks also to the great masters of many traditions whom I have had the great fortune to meet and learn from.

My sincere thanks to Dr. D.V.R. Seshadri, Professor at ISB, Hyderabad, for writing the foreword and Ganesh Chella of Totus Consulting for writing the book review and also to Raghu Krishnamoorthy (former head of HR at GE, USA and a coach, speaker, faculty member, and thought leader), Hema Ravichandar (former head of HR at Infosys and strategic HR advisor), and Dr. Kannan Srinivasan (Director, CSIR – Central Salt and Marine Chemicals Research Institute, Council of Scientific and Industrial Research) for their advance review of the book and their suggestions and comments which helped to polish this book and make it more readable. My thanks also to my long-term business partner Mrs. Vijayalakshmi Rao (currently an independent consultant and coach) for her valuable and insightful comments.

Finally, any shortcoming in this study is purely mine and I look forward to comments from readers to improve the book in future versions.

R. Sivadas
rsivadas@gmail.com
December 2020

About the Author

R. Sivadas is a serial entrepreneur and business leader with particular strengths in entrepreneurship, innovation, managing investments, and business development. He completed his postgraduation in management in 1983 from the Indian Institute of Management, Ahmedabad, India, and until 2012 he was the Co-Founder and Managing Director of Scope e-Knowledge Center, Chennai, a global content provider in the scientific and technical space. Scope was acquired in 2011 by Quatrro, an Indian company funded by US-based venture fund Olympia Capital.

He was a key member of the team that led Scope e-Knowledge Center, one of the first Knowledge Process Offshoring players in India in the publishing and intellectual property space. He has successfully completed three rounds of exits in entrepreneurial ventures, the latest being the sale of RSI Content Solutions to Orbis, USA (February 2018). In the information area, he has worked with multinationals, large Indian private corporations, government institutions, and not for profits in areas such as market research, consulting, building and promotion of e-content, e-commerce, and electronic databases.

Sivadas is keenly interested in badminton, trekking, and yoga and he spends significant amount of time in learning from nature and in exploring the inner realms through meditation. He is a strong advocate of yoga and meditation for all-round personal growth. He has authored a book on entrepreneurship *Failure to Millionaire: How I Created a Successful Company and How You Can Too!* that was published by Sage in December 2015 and is currently available on Kindle and Amazon.

Table of Contents

1 Current Social and Business Environment Post Covid and the Changing Role of the Knowledge Worker

Society needs a return to spiritual values – not to offset the material but to make it fully productive
– Peter Drucker

Peter Drucker, considered by many as one of the foremost thinkers and writers on modern management, further wrote,

> "However remote its realization for the great mass on mankind, there is today the promise of material abundance or at least of material sufficiency. In the current age of terror, persecution and mass murder, a hard shell of moral callousness may be necessary to survival. Without it we might yield to paralyzing despair. But moral dumbness is also a terrible disease of mind and soul and a terrible danger."

Drucker wrote that humanity "needs the deep experience that Thou and I are one, which all higher religions share."

In his book *Post-Capitalist Society*, published in 1993, Drucker wrote of the "existential goals" of redemption, self-renewal, spiritual growth, goodness, and virtue. However, much earlier, in his book *The Age of Discontinuity*, published on 1969, he had written about this existential challenge: "The society of organizations forces the individual to ask of himself: 'Who am I?' 'What do I want to be?' 'What do I want to put into life and what do I want to get out of it?'" Probably he was the first management thinker to take spirituality and existential questions out of the pure spiritual realms and question their relevance in the management domain.

Drucker wrote about this in his book *Landmarks of Tomorrow*, published on 1959, a tribute to his farsightedness and clarity of thought in the face of the changing role of the worker from a production-oriented person to that of a knowledge-oriented one. He understood that the world of business is one filled with stress and ultra-competition, and under its pressures and compulsions it is quite easy to succumb to the temptations of the material without any regard to the development of the persona. Actions rooted in the basic motives of greed and selfishness alone without any regard to moral values have real-world effects, for example, the financial crisis in 2008 which strained economies around the world and wiped of trillions of dollars of wealth with devastating consequences across the world. The crisis has had a negative impact on millions of people across the world and thrown people into drugs and alcohol abuse, suicides, family break-ups, and devastation. Something similar and probably far more severe in its impact is happening around the globe at present in this pandemic.

In a recent survey after the Covid outbreak, it was found that approximately 67% of respondents experienced medium to high level of stress due to the coronavirus pandemic. Approximately 32% reported feeling nervous, scared, or stressed on most of the days. In June 2020, more than 40% of entrepreneurs reported experiencing a rise in their stress level during the lockdown. The reasons for stress and anxiety are not hard to guess. Entrepreneurs and managers are reporting heightened distress and worry about how to manage their companies with the new norms of work from home and severe limitations on travel being implemented across industries. There is immense pressure to keep employees engaged while maintaining productivity besides heightened business issues such as orders and collections.

There is a question mark on survival and the tough decisions one needs to take including downsizing or closing down businesses besides dealing with government authorities. This leads to a mental health crisis of sorts for many entrepreneurs, increasing doubts and anxiety in some, while others have gone into denial mode. Many of them are experiencing burn out and mental fatigue due to the exponential increase in uncertainties and a lack of control. In addition, there are acceleration in new technologies, rise in competition, the global nature of competition, quarterly watch on results, increasing number of upstarts who disrupt existing and hitherto stable business models (e.g. Uber, Oyo, Air B&B, IOT-based businesses, etc.). All these factors have an impact on managers at an individual level who are under the stress of coping with constant change, producing results continuously with the need to balance their professional and personal lives.

In this context, the story of John Mackey, co-founder and CEO of Whole Foods Market, who has led the natural and organic grocer to a US$15.7 billion Fortune 500 company with more than 460 stores and 87,000 team members in three countries, is worth reading. The company has been included in "100 Best Companies to Work For" list by Fortune magazine for 20 consecutive years and John Mackey has been recognized as one of the Fortune's "World's 50 Greatest Leaders," besides several other awards.

His philosophy was founded on

(i) Energy and vitality are critical – "You cannot be lazy."
(ii) A strong desire to be excellent. Excellent leaders strive for excellence in everything they choose to do.
(iii) Good physical and mental health.
(iv) Honour – Need to uphold high standards.

Mackey and Rene Lawson collected US$45,000 from family and friends and borrowed US$10,000 to open a small natural foods store called SaferWay in Austin, Texas in 1978. When the couple were evicted from their apartment for storing food products in it, they decided to live at the store. Since the store was zoned for commercial use, there was no shower stall, so they bathed using a water hose attached to their dishwasher. Two years later, they brought in partners who owned another grocery store and formed Whole. In 1981, they had to deal with a 100-year flood in Austin. Rene had to swim out of the store that day. In Mackey's words, "Whole Foods should have died that day. That was when I learned about stakeholders." Many people helped them stay in business. A banker co-signed on the loan without approval because of his trust on the couple. Mackey moved to Boulder in 1999 to run WholePeople.com. Then the internet bubble popped and this resulted in the failure of the website. When he moved back to Austin, Texas, a coup was afoot. One of his trusted senior leaders was trying to get Mackey fired. Mackey walked through the nearest Whole Foods while preparing to tell the board why he should keep his job. In his words, "I get a super high touring that store." Touring the stores helped him feel the pulse of the company and this is when he realized that this was the love of his life and this was his purpose. That conviction helped him keep his job by convincing the Board of Directors and he learnt to cultivate and build relationships with his board through it. He later wrote a book in which he defined his idea of a conscious leader as one who had

- Vision and virtue – put purpose first, lead with love.
- Mindset and strategy – find win–win solutions. Innovate and create value.
- People and culture – constantly evolve the team. Regularly revitalize, continually learn and grow.
- Constantly revitalize yourself:
    - Sleep well
    - Eat healthy food
    - Exercise.

It is completely possible to recharge one's mental and physical well-being during a stressful situation through meditation, through a quick nap or even through the visualization of what makes one happy. However, it needs some understanding of the fact that there are ways to de-stress naturally and some disciplines to put them into practice. This book will cover some of these processes in the chapters that follow.

There are some interesting comments in the World Bank Report 2010 which impact the kind of skills that entrepreneurs, managers, and workers need to survive and do good in the foreseeable future:

- "Machines are coming to take our jobs" has been a concern for hundreds of years
- Innovation and technological progress have caused disruption, but they have created more prosperity than they have destroyed.We are riding a new wave of uncertainty as the pace of innovation continues to accelerate and technology affects every part of our lives.
- Robots are taking over thousands of routine tasks and will eliminate many low-skill jobs in advanced economies and developing countries.
- Technology is creating opportunities, paving the way for new and altered jobs, increasing productivity and improving the delivery of public services.
- It is important to understand that many children currently in primary school will work in jobs as adults which do not even exist today.
- Many jobs at present, and many more in the near future, will require specific skills – a combination of technological know-how, problem-solving, and critical thinking as well as soft skills such as perseverance, collaboration, and empathy.
- The days of staying in one job, or with one company, for decades are waning. In the gig economy, workers will likely have many gigs over the course of their careers which means they will have to be lifelong learners.

Some of the features of the current wave of technological progress are as follows:

- Digital technologies allow firms to scale up or down quickly, blurring the boundaries of firms and challenging traditional production patterns.
- New business models – digital platform firms – are evolving from local start-ups to global behemoths, often with few employees or tangible assets.
- The rise of platform marketplaces allows the effects of technology to reach more people more quickly than ever before.
- This "scale without mass" brings economic opportunity to millions of people.

It follows that three types of skills are increasingly important in labour markets:

- Advanced cognitive skills such as complex problem-solving.
- Socio-behavioural skills such as teamwork.
- Skill combinations that are predictive of adaptability such as reasoning and self-efficacy.

Building these skills requires strong foundations and lifelong learning. This has an impact both at the individual level and at the organizational level. Currently, at the individual level, stress, anxiety, depression, etc. have an impact on health at heightened levels. In addition, there are issues, such as lack of concentration and anger management issues, which have an impact at the workplace. The other issues are unannounced absenteeism and employee attrition, all of which have a negative impact on the organization.

In this context, mindfulness as a tool to build inner resilience and inner mastery has become quite popular in the United States and elsewhere to tackle issues such as attention deficit and stress. A large number of corporates across the spectrum have adopted mindfulness as a tool to tackle these issues. A lot of scientific study and research has been done and continues to be done to determine the impact of mindfulness and to understand how mindfulness is beneficial at the workplace. This is evident with well-known institutions such as Harvard, Stanford, Berkeley, MIT, Columbia, Drucker School of Management, Claremont, etc., offering courses in mindfulness as part of their MBA curriculum. Corporates such as Google, Ford, Ebay, General Mills, Cargill, Facebook, Aetna, Target, Hearst Publications to name a few have adopted mindfulness programmes as part of their corporate training within their organizations. Diverse organizations as mentioned earlier have one thing in common – progressive managements – as they realize that their continued well-being rests on motivated and well-functioning executives and not just on external systems and processes. After all we live in a knowledge economy where the value of organizations is primarily defined by the quality and productivity of their employees.

We stand on the brink of a technological revolution which will fundamentally alter the way we live, work, and relate to one another. In its scale, scope, and complexity, the transformation will be unlike anything humankind has experienced earlier. At present, we are in the midst of the Fourth Industrial Revolution built on the digital revolution that we have seen over the last few decades and this is characterized by a fusion of technologies that blurs the lines between the physical, digital, and biological spheres. The speed of current breakthroughs has no historical precedent and it evolves at an exponential rather than a linear pace, disrupting processes and industries across countries. The possibilities of billions of people connected by mobile devices, with unprecedented processing power, storage capacity, and access to knowledge, are unlimited; something that we see with apps such as WhatsApp, Twitter, Facebook, Google, etc., where cutting across national boundaries they are able to influence the way people think, speak, vote and live. Virtually every area of life has been impacted. These possibilities will be compounded by emerging technology innovations in fields such as artificial intelligence, robotics, the Internet of Things, autonomous vehicles, three-dimensional (3-D) printing, nanotechnology, biotechnology, materials science, energy storage, and quantum computing.

CHALLENGES AND OPPORTUNITIES

While these innovations and progress have the potential to raise global income levels and improve the quality of life for populations around the world, they also bring with them several challenges. To date, those who have gained the most from them have been consumers who are able to afford and access the digital world. Technology has made possible new products and services which increase the efficiency and pleasure of our personal lives. Ordering a cab, booking a flight, buying a product, making a payment, listening to music, watching a film, or playing a game – any of these can currently be done remotely. This ability has come in very useful in these days of the global pandemic which has minimized the impact of a large number of knowledge workers unable to move out of their homes. Most employees have been able to work from home and the issue has been more in terms of managing the "work from home" and its resultant issues rather than not being able to work at all.

At the same time, as the economists Erik Brynjolfsson and Andrew McAfee have pointed out, the revolution could yield greater inequality, particularly in its potential to disrupt labour markets. This will also possibly lead to greater social inequity and also create tensions and worries in the labour market because of the pace of change and existing technologies becoming obsolete.

However, I am convinced of one thing that in the future, talent, more than capital, will represent the critical factor of production leading to an asymmetry in compensation. This will give rise to a job market highly segregated into "low-skill/low-pay" and "high-skill/high-pay" segments, which in turn will lead to an increase in social tensions.

Technology will also probably change not only what we do but also who we are. It will affect our identity and all the issues associated with it: our sense of privacy, notions of ownership, consumption patterns, the time we devote to work and leisure, and how we develop our careers, cultivate our skills, meet people, and nurture relationships. This will also impact health and well-being in a big way and the way we manage them. For example, most millennials probably have hundreds if not thousands of "friends" linked to them on Facebook or other social media such as Instagram but very few whom they can trust and pour their hearts out to face to face in times of need.

This means that change is only constant. Here is a story that articulates change which I think brings out the issue of change very well.

> Prior to 2008, the British cycling team had last won a gold medal in 1908 and had never won the Tour de France. The management were convinced that they needed a massive change to taste success. In 2003, they appointed Dave Brailsford as the Performance Director to make a total change in the way the team performed and operated. He came up with an idea called "the aggregation of marginal gains" which basically meant breaking everything down and put it back and during the process try to make improvements of 1% in all the parts. The sum total would be significant change. The process involved looking at every single thing that they could think of; the seats on their bikes; putting alcohol on their tyres to get better traction; getting all to choose the right pillow for themselves and to take it with them while traveling so they slept better. They even painted the interiors of their team trucks white so that they could see every speck of dirt and ensure that everything was clean and spotless.
>
> Five years later, in 2008, the British cycling team dominated the Beijing Olympics. They won 60% of all the gold medals and at the London Olympics, in 2012, they ended up with nine Olympic records and seven world records. Their success continued through the Rio Olympics in 2016 where they won two-third of the gold medals.

The story articulates the importance of understanding the need for and showing the flexibility and willingness to change as a prerequisite for coping with change.

The development of flexibility and a willingness to embrace change will make one a more valuable member of the organization to which he/she belongs. The other skills one needs to develop are as follows:

- Building skills and continuous learning.
- Adapting to change frequently requires the effective use of one's acquired skills. In some cases, adapting to change will call for the use of other skills as well – skills that one might not yet have mastered or even begun to acquire.
- The ability to adapt is the key.
- Embracing technological change and learning how to use it for one's own benefit.
- Increasing one's speed of response. Greater opportunities come to organizations that can respond quickly.
- The ability to live with ambiguity and uncertainty. Most people do not like ambiguity and uncertainty that are major sources of anxiety but also facts of life in this fast-changing world.

This means that everyone – entrepreneur, manager, or knowledge worker – has to build resilience and inner strength to deal with change. This calls for:

- Continuous lifelong learning.
- Strengthening the mind to deal with uncertainty.
- Learning how to control one's emotions and deal with worry and stresses, in fact thrive on them.

The place to start is oneself: understanding oneself and making oneself robust and physically, mentally, emotionally, intellectually, and spiritually strong.

UNDERSTANDING CHANGE

This means that the workers' "mind" and of course their overall well-being needs to be the centre of attention. In the words of Roberto Assagioli, the Italian psychiatrist and pioneer in the fields of humanistic and transpersonal psychology, "Only the development of his inner powers can offset the dangers inherent in man's losing control of the tremendous natural forces at his disposal and becoming the victim of his own achievements." Hence the imperative is to ensure that the workers' physical, mental, and psychological well-being is looked after through techniques such as gyms and sports facilities in case of physical well-being, and meditation, breathing, and mindfulness programmes for mental well-being. In addition, the workers' values and outlook need to be aligned to that of the management/founders. This "self-management" where the workers are trained to help themselves is now supported by the whole lot of research on the brain, neurochemistry, and neuropsychology.

Most of the current research in this area focus on "attention" or "self-awareness." While this study is a good start and has tremendous benefits, in most cases, this practice is not sustained because of several factors, most notably because it is not complete in itself. Buddhist monks are trained to the practice of "attention" but then they spend a major part of their lives in such training and it becomes natural to them. Hence, I have attempted to expand this practice along with some insights to the reasons why some supplementary practices will be most beneficial. Wherever there is research I have tried to link it up; however much more research is called for to understand why and how these practices are beneficial in aiding attention.

As the famous basketball coach George Raveling says, one of his greatest learnings in more than six decades of his association with the sport is the importance of self-leadership – "You must take care of yourself before trying to lead others."

KEY TAKEAWAY

This chapter laid the foundation of the social and business environment at present and the importance of emotional resilience in a post Covid world. While we have emphasized the knowledge worker, this is applicable virtually to everyone as we live in a knowledge world driven by digital technology which is put to use in varying degrees by almost everyone whether for personal or official use. People from all walks of life, whether a student, a housewife, an executive, or a professional, need to build resilience and inner strength to deal with change since change is the order of the day.

This chapter explained the rationale for:

- Continuous lifelong learning.
- Strengthening the mind to deal with uncertainty.
- Learning how to control one's emotions and deals with worry and stresses, in fact thrive on them.

The next chapter will examine some enduring leadership principles based on the lives of some of the acknowledged great leaders who have impacted many lives. We will analyse why they were successful as leaders and what kind of internal skills did they consciously build.

2 Understanding Enduring Leadership Principles

The term "leadership" has many meanings and almost every person who has been successful has his or her own definition of leadership. Here is a story that outlines the nature of leadership.

Tenali Raman or Tenali Ramalingam was a minister in the court of the king of Vijayanagar, Krishnadevaraya in southern India. Tenali Raman was a great scholar of several languages that included Marathi, Tamil, and Kannada. He was popular all over the country for his wit and great sense of humour. Stories about Tenali Raman and his practical jokes on everyone around him including distinguished fellow poets and the emperor himself, are very famous all over the world for his wisdom and statesmanship.

The king loved to test his courtiers frequently and very often he would throw up tough riddles and challenges to them, rewarding the winners handsomely who could crack them. The king's challenges were difficult. After burning their fingers a few times, the majority of the courtiers quit participating and became mere spectators of such events. Only Tenali Raman, the brilliant minister, continued to take part and win. "Here is the challenge for the day," proclaimed King Krishnadevaraya as soon as the court had assembled one day, "In the centre of the court you can see that two identical earthen pots are hung. One of them has gold coins and the other is empty. If you accept the challenge and identify the pot with gold, it is yours to keep. If you pick the wrong one, you will be banished from the court for two months and should pay a fine in gold coins. Let us see who is the cleverest among you."

For this challenge also, Tenali Raman alone came forward. He spent some time circling under the hung pots closely examining them. The pots were absolutely identical in shape, size, and artistic design. It seemed impossible to guess what was inside them just by how they looked. Then suddenly Tenali Raman walked to a nearby guard, borrowed his spear, came over, and broke one of the pots confidently. Gold coins showered on him. The king was impressed not only with Tenali Raman's intelligence but also with the confident gesture of breaking the pot. Being confident in one's abilities is just as important as having those abilities. "Well done, Tenali Raman," said the beaming Krishnadevaraya, "now tell us how you did it?" "Beloved King, please forgive me for saying that this was the easiest of all the challenges. That is why I was able to confidently break the correct pot. The trick was not to look at the pots themselves but the ropes on which they were suspended. The tension in the taut ropes of the heavier pot was obvious." So what lesson have we learnt here?

The first lesson is, as leaders, sometimes we need to focus our attention not on the problem but around it to discover the solution. We get (so) overwhelmed by the magnitude of the problem and the myriad solution options that we fail to notice the "taut ropes," the straight simple solution that might just be staring us in the face. Every problem can have multiple possible solutions and it only requires change in perception and application to discover the most viable and simplistic solution that always resides within the problem itself. The second lesson is one's self-confidence and the ability to operate the mind even in the midst of looming dangers and stresses.

Here are some interesting observations on leadership.

A supervisor's comment on an employee evaluation: "He's never been very successful. When opportunity knocks, he complains about the noise."

> You do not lead by hitting people over the head – that's assault, not leadership. – Dwight Eisenhower

> A leader is best when people barely know he exists, not so good when people obey and acclaim him, worse when they despise him. But of a good leader who talks little when his work is done, his aim fulfilled, they will say: We did it ourselves. – Lao-Tzu

Leadership is defined in myriad ways and one of the best ways to learn about it is to look at the lives of acknowledged leaders and study the attributes that made them great leaders, as outlined by their biographers.

So, let us look at Mahatma Gandhi and Nelson Mandela from the field of politics, Steve Jobs and Bill Gates from the field of business, and Swami Vivekananda and the Dalai Lama from the field of spirituality. Their qualities are to some extent subjective, but below is the list of top 5–6 qualities of each leader as given by their biographers or mentioned most often.

MAHATMA GANDHI

Mahatma Gandhi or Mohandas Karamchand Gandhi, as everyone knows, was a lawyer, politician, social activist, and writer, who became the leader of the nationalist movement against the British rule. As such, he came to be considered the Father of the Nation and is internationally esteemed for his doctrine of non-violent protest or Satyagraha to achieve political and social progress. He had a firm belief in and asked his followers to employ non-cooperation, non-violence, and peaceful resistance as their "weapons" in the struggle against the British Raj. He was widely popular among both Hindus and Muslims in India. His birthday, 2nd October, is commemorated in India as Gandhi Jayanti, a national holiday, and worldwide as the International Day of Non-Violence.

Leadership as exemplified by Gandhi is the art of putting others first and giving of oneself to a cause greater than one's own progress or profit. In order to become a fit instrument of "giving of self to others," one must first undergo a process of complete self-purification and self-transformation following strict self-discipline. Self-discipline involves three related aspects of self-control: the ability to resist temptation, the ability to tolerate delay of gratification, and the imposing of strict standards of accomplishment upon oneself. Essentially, it entails the conservation of energy so that it can be rechannelized in harnessing self-awareness. Such self-discipline became the hallmark of Gandhi's pedagogy of transformation of character and he achieved it through various practices such as prayer, vows, fasting, and confession. In his own words: "The call to lead India did not come to me in the nature of a sudden realization. I prepared for it by fasting and self-discipline."

Described below are some of Gandhi's major leadership traits as described by biographers:

1. *A shared mission*: One of Gandhi's biographers put it very well when he said, "Gandhi lost himself in the service of others." A leader needs to have a mission that is synch with strongly held values. Holding the trust of your followers is extremely crucial. Once your mission exists, then your followers and fans will also exist. For Mahatma Gandhi, the biggest mission was serving others and striving for the freedom of the nation, and this is the reason he was able to attract millions of followers, who trusted him, and believed him.

2. *Strength of character*: The strength of character is exemplified by traits such as honesty, non-violence, and truthfulness among others. These were the Mahatma's hallmarks, something that he based his whole life on. A great leader always leads with an exemplary life that echoes his ideals based on personal traits. Gandhi always maintained that, "If Wealth is lost, nothing is lost; If Health is lost, something is lost; but If Character is lost, everything is lost." Gandhi sacrificed his thriving law practice and adopted a simple life to live among the millions who lived in poverty during his freedom struggle. At present, we see modern leaders cajoling the masses with promises that they never intend to keep; let alone practicing what they preach in their own lives. "You must be the change you wish to see in the world."
3. *Faith in oneself and persistence*: "First they ignore you, then they laugh at you, then they fight you, then you win." A critical success for Gandhi was the support he got across the nation and in the international community. A significant part of this was due to his extraordinary persistence once he had articulated his vision and his methods. His determination in following through on what he preached was often at a cost of his own well-being. Gandhi was insulted, jailed and beaten. But still, the biggest weapon he possessed was of persistence. He just refused to give in and continued his fight against the Britishers.
4. *Self-mastery and control of mind*: "Will-power, control of anger and negativity. The weak can never forgive, for forgiveness is the attribute of the strong." Gandhi shared a great leadership thought, here which is about controlling one's emotions and sentiments. Both anger and intolerance are the greatest negative forces, and they can destroy a person and hamper all leadership efforts.
5. *Self-discipline*: Happiness is what one thinks, what one says, and what one does in harmony. Gandhi believed that challenging his self-discipline heightened his commitment to achieve his goals. He was a focused leader who had resolve and persistence in achieving his goals. His objective was to free India and he was prepared to die in the process. He did extraordinary things to improve his discipline and his commitment, which are elaborated in most of his biographies.

In addition, one of the key attributes he gave a lot of importance to was health. He always maintained that "It is health that is real wealth and not pieces of gold and silver." Gandhi attributed health as a major factor for his success. And herein lies a great success mantra for the leader: Unless one focuses on his/her health, he/she cannot achieve much. By health, he meant both physical and mental health and well-being.

To summarize, the following are the major leadership attributes exemplified by Gandhi:

1. A shared mission
2. Strength of character
3. Faith in oneself and persistence
4. Self-mastery and control of mind
5. Self-discipline
6. Health.

NELSON MANDELA

Nelson Mandela was born into the royal Tembu family in July 1918 in the village of Qunu, in Umtata in the south-eastern Transkei region of South Africa and rose from relative rural obscurity to challenge the apartheid government. He spent 27 years in jail from 1962 for his attempts to overthrow the country's white-minority government before being freed in 1990. In 1993, Mandela and South African President F.W. de Klerk were jointly awarded the Nobel Peace Prize for their efforts to dismantle the country's apartheid system. For generations to come, Mandela will be a source of inspiration for civil rights activists worldwide.

He led the African National Congress (ANC) liberation organization in negotiations with the National Party to secure South Africa's first inclusive election in 1994 and became South Africa's first black president in 1994. After just a single term in office, he stepped down as president in 1999. In retirement, Mandela focused his energy on his new role as a roving elder statesman and leading HIV/AIDS campaigner before retiring from public life in 2004. One of the most inspirational leaders ever, he became a larger than life person when he forgave his oppressors and looked forward to building a new South Africa based on principles of equality and justice without harping on past injustices. In real life, one rues a bad day at work or a run-in with his/her boss but in case of Mandela his leaders put him in prison for life. It was his ability to persevere that kept him going despite punishment designed to break his spirit, be it back-breaking work in a lime quarry or solitary confinement during his prison term.

> As I walked out the door toward the gate that would lead to my freedom, I knew if I didn't leave my bitterness and hatred behind, I'd still be in prison. – Nelson Mandela

Mandela demonstrated remarkable leadership qualities. Apart from being a man of peace and showing the world what it was to forgive, similar to Gandhi, he also focused on goals and a mission far beyond himself.

His biographers have identified the following to be his main leadership principles:

1. *Be brave and courageous*, or learn to put up a front. Courage is not the absence of fear but the triumph over it. The brave man is not one who does not feel afraid, but he who conquers that fear. Mandela took on the apartheid regime and went about leading protests and groups without showing any fear. He learned that it pays to be fearless, from people who sacrificed their lives, despite being afraid, for freedom. It is not necessary to always suppress emotions, but it helps to express it in a way that provides comfort to the people who follow them.
2. When the going gets tough, *persist*. "The greatest glory in living lies not in never falling but in rising every time we fall." Mandela was speaking about the power of persistence, more specifically the power to get up day after day and fight all over again. This finally helps one attain success and glory.
3. *Lead from behind* and put others in front. "It is better to lead from behind and put others in front, especially when you celebrate victory when nice things occur. You can take the front line when there is danger. Then people will appreciate your leadership. A leader is like a shepherd. He stays behind the flock, letting the most nimble go out ahead whereupon the others follow, not realising that all along they are being directed from behind" – *Long Walk to Freedom: The Autobiography of Nelson Mandela.*
4. *Spread happiness through one's team* with a smile. "Tread softly. Breathe peacefully. Laugh hysterically." A research paper published in the *Journal of Experimental Psychology* noted that connecting with others, even strangers, increases personal happiness. Some of the ways to spread smiles in the office include

   - Greet coworkers with a *smile.*
   - Praise the efforts of colleagues.
   - Surprise coworkers with some gesture of kindness.

5. *Focus on converting the enemy* into a frenemy. "If you want to make peace with your enemy, you have to work with your enemy. Then he becomes your partner." Accepting that there are differences is the first step to reducing or resolving them. The more proactive one is towards understanding the other persons' point of view, and the other person will himself/herself see the need to at least come to a "workable" relationship. Spending time to understand a person is therefore very important. It also helps in solving the ego hassles and creates an environment that is of collaboration rather than confusion. However, by asking one's enemies to be part of his/her plan, asking them for opinions, and involving them in his/her ideas, he/she might be able to pull off that project far more easily.

To summarize, the major leadership attributes exemplified by Mandela are as follows:

1. A shared mission
2. Brave and courageous
3. Faith in oneself and persistence
4. Lead from behind
5. Spread a smile (that also means a total control of one's emotions)
6. Convert one's enemy to a frenemy.

BILL GATES

Entrepreneur and businessman Bill Gates and his business partner Paul Allen founded and built the world's largest software business, Microsoft, through technological innovation, keen business strategy, and aggressive business tactics. In this process, Gates became one of the richest men in the world. At Harvard, a 20-year-old Gates came up with an impressive solution to the so-called "pancake sorting" problem in math which had stood for 30 years. But when his professor called him and said that his solution would be published in an academic paper, he did not care and he had already gone off to found Microsoft.

Brad Silverberg, formerly a Microsoft SVP of many years, once wrote, "Shortly after I had joined Microsoft in 1990, Bill, I and a few others on the Windows team were flying to New York from Seattle for some customer meetings. This was shortly after the launch of windows 3.0 though this was 25 years ago. Microsoft was a public and prosperous company. Yet, company policy was that executives flew coach and there was Bill sitting in coach in a middle seat. It didn't matter to him, he spent the whole flight reading. It made a big impression on me, a new employee, seeing Bill lead by example."

He stepped down from executive positions at Microsoft in 2014. Since then, he has been focusing on his charitable foundation "The Bill and Melinda Gates Foundation."

When Gates and Paul Allen started Microsoft, their vision of "a computer on every desktop and in every home" seemed far-fetched to most of the people. At present that vision is a reality in many parts of the world, and personal technology is an integral part of society.

His biographers indicate the following as his key leadership skills:

1. *Focus*: Knowing something is much different than having wisdom. Gates focused on one thing he knows best, which is software. "If you don't build your dreams, someone else will hire you to build theirs."
2. *Passionate*: If something is worth doing, then it is worth doing it to the best of one's ability.
3. *Take risks*: Determine a goal and never stop. Take risks – persistence – "To win big, sometimes you have to take big risks." Failure does not mean that one will never succeed.
4. *Creativity*: Many people followed Gates because they knew he could help them transform themselves into better leaders too.
5. *Caring*: Pursue success, but remember those less fortunate. From those to whom much is given, much is expected. He is also one of the most prolific givers to philanthropic causes in the world today. That caring attitude was also present in the workplace, making sure that people had the best possible opportunity to find success if they wanted it.

STEVE JOBS

Steve Jobs was adopted by Paul and Clara Jobs, a lower middle-class couple, who moved to the suburban city of Mountain View a couple of years later.

The Santa Clara county, south of the Bay Area, became known as Silicon Valley in the early 1950s after the sprouting of a myriad of semiconductor companies. As a result, young Jobs grew up in a neighbourhood of engineers working on electronics and other gizmos in their garages on weekends. This shaped his interest in the field as he grew up. At age 13, he met 18-year-old Stephen Wozniak, an electronics whiz kid. Together they started Apple Computers in 1979 with a view to bring computing to the common man. Jobs had a roller-coaster ride at Apple, from where he was ousted in 1985. He was reinstated as CEO in 1997 when Apple acquired NeXT, the company Jobs had founded post his ouster from Apple.

Jobs told his biographer Walter Isaacson that he was so exhausted in the days after he returned to Apple, he could not speak when he came home at night (he was also running another successful company Pixar simultaneously). He reviewed every team at Apple and asked them to justify why they were important to the future of the company. If they could not justify, their product would get cancelled, and there was a high probability they would have to leave too. Jobs also brought with him his executive team from NeXT and installed them in key positions. Jobs unveiled his first great product post return in 1988, the iMac the first for Apple since the original Macintosh in 1984. It took the PC World by storm because of its design and ease of navigation. Design innovations continued throughout 1998 and 1999 with the coloured iMacs and the iBook, Apple's consumer notebook. After being in charge for 3 years, Jobs had brought Apple back to its status of cool tech icon.

Jobs was an innovator who pursued the nature and enlightenment of life through Zen meditation which refers to the performance of mental concentration that leads to the state of enlightenment by refining his mind and unifying the spirit. That kind of meditation had a big impact on his life and the products he made. His entire approach was solely aesthetics of minimalism and intense concentration. That was his uniqueness. That was all imbibed from Zen meditation.

What did Jobs obtain through meditation? Here are excerpts from his own writings and speeches:

1. *Courage to follow intuition. Seeking the voice within me.*

   "Everybody's time is limited. Don't waste your time trying to live somebody else's life. The noise from someone else's voice, make sure it does not cover/overturn your own inner voice. What is most important is that you need to have courage to follow your mind and intuition. You already know what your mind and intuition want. Everything outside of that is secondary."

   This is what 50-year-old Jobs said in 2005 after he fought off pancreatic cancer and dramatically came back, giving a graduation speech at the podium at Stanford University. More than anybody else, he was a person who followed the voice of his mind and intuition, not from his head but from his heart. The products such as Apple, Macintosh computer, Pixar, ipod, iphone, and the iPad came from Jobs following his heart and intuition. When others around him were telling it would not work, he pursued his ideas through his assurance of his intuition.

   Jobs knew that intuitive understanding and awareness was more important than abstract thinking and intelligent logic analysis. His intuitive insights came from his meditation.

   Evaluation of others, calculations of profit and loss, and fear-like noises are removed. Zen meditation is defined as time and space where one can remain quiet and sincere. Jobs's meditation was solely time to know and meet his true self.

2. *Aesthetics of simplicity. Just discard everything and leave only the essence.*

   In his words, "Completion is, not when there is nothing more to add, but rather when there is nothing left to remove. Simplicity is harder than complication. To make your thinking clear and simple requires a lot of effort. When you reach the level of being able to think simply, you can move mountains."

Jobs, not only in his life but also in the products he made, pursued simplicity. When Apple's iPhone and iPod were introduced, the keyword he always used was "simple." All innovations led by Apple are born from the dedication to simplicity in life. The common theme out of the several reasons why Apple was able to succeed was simplicity. Apple's strongest pro was to make complicated into simple, so users found it comfortable and easy to use. But just as Jobs also expressed, simplicity is something very difficult to do. To make it simple, one has to be able to understand the deeper essence of the product's true properties. To be able to see that essence, one needs intuition and to stay focused. Jobs stated that he had these abilities through Zen meditation.

3. *Unconventional, every moment he breaks frames.*

Jobs lived a life of challenges to common sense and customs in many areas. He refused to be still and even if he failed, he wanted to move forward, constantly pushing to innovate, always trying to evolve. As people age, they get stuck in their ways and their thoughts create a pattern that is difficult to break. Breaking this pattern needs the ability to witness and understand it and not be swayed by these thoughts. Jobs was able to do that simply. In Jobs's own words, "If you sit still and look within, you will see our minds are unstable and restless. But as time passes, the waves crashing in the mind will calm down. Then this creates a margin that can detect something more subtle. At that moment, our intuition kicks in and one can see the world more clearly and become more faithful to the present. You start to see things more clearly and be in the present more. Your mind just slows down, and you see a tremendous expanse in the moment. You see so much more than you could see before. This is the cultivation of the heart which needs to be constantly trained."

His leadership skills were centred around the following attributes:

1. *Simplicity*: This has been one of his mantras. Simple can be harder than complex. One has to work hard to get his/her thinking clean to make it simple. But it is worth in the end because once one gets there, he/she can move mountains. "Simplicity is the ultimate sophistication," "it takes a lot of hard work," he said, "to make something simple, to truly understand the underlying challenges and come up with elegant solutions."
2. *Focus*: Focus was ingrained in Jobs's personality and had been honed by his Zen training. He relentlessly filtered out what he considered distractions. Jobs's Zen like ability to focus was accompanied by the related instinct to simplify things by zeroing in on their essence and eliminating unnecessary components. Here is an interesting anecdote that illustrates this point.

   Once when he was doing the iPhone, Jobs decided that he did not want plastic, he wanted really tough glass on it. There were not many who made glass that was tough like what he wanted. Finally, someone told him that one possibility was Corning as they were making all of the glass in China for the storefronts. So, he flew to Corning, New York, and sat there in front of the CEO, Wendell Weeks. Jobs told Weeks the kind of glass he wanted. Weeks told Jobs that they once created a type of process that created something called Gorilla Glass. Jobs apparently interrupted and tried to tell Weeks how to make really strong glass. Wendell got a bit ruffled and told Jobs to shut up and listen to him as he was the glass maker. Jobs, to his credit, shut up and listened and Weeks described a process to make Gorilla Glass. Jobs was delighted and told Weeks that in 6 months he wanted a million pieces. Weeks then told him he was sorry but that he had actually never made any and furthermore they had no factory in which

Gorilla glass could be made. They had developed this process but had never built a manufacturing facility for it. Jobs looked at him and said what he had said to Woz, 20–30 years earlier: "Don't be afraid, you can do it." In Weeks words, "I just sat there and looked at the guy." He kept saying, "Don't be afraid. You can do this."

Jobs's fierceness and concentration abilities were obvious. First he prioritized, then focused his attention, and filtered out distractions. If something caught his attention, he focused on it without hesitation. He excluded some buttons to make the machine simpler, removed some features to make the software simpler, removed some options, and made the interface simple. He believed his ability to concentrate and his simplicity were related to his Zen meditation.

In 1997, Jobs managed Apple that was going down a bad path and as soon as he became the CEO, he decreased the number of products Apple was making and focused on only four computers. At that time, Apple was creating 40 plus products, and many people were against it saying it was impossible, but Jobs rearranged it to focus on the core. Unlike what people predicted, Jobs's simplicity was a big success. After Apple made a comeback, he made a 10 billion dollar debt into a 4 billion dollar profit.

This was because he knew that staying focused while getting rid of the unnecessary was the way to live a simple life. To decide whether something is essential or not and shrug off those that are not. This is the strong point of simplicity and focus. Meditation helps to build that ability.

3. *Take responsibility end to end*: Part of Jobs's compulsion to take responsibility for what he called "the whole widget" stemmed from his personality, which was very controlling. But it was also driven by his passion for perfection and making elegant products.

   Jobs often taught in parables. One such lesson was called the "Difference Between the Janitor and the Vice President," and it is a sermon Jobs delivered every time an executive reached the vice president level.

   Jobs imagined that his garbage was not regularly being emptied in his office, and when he asked the janitor for the reason, the excuse he got was that the locks had been changed and he did not have a key. In Jobs's words, "this is an acceptable excuse coming from someone who empties trash bins for a living." The janitor gets to explain why something went wrong. Senior people do not. "When you're the janitor," Jobs used to repeatedly tell incoming VPs, that "reasons matter." He asserted that, "Somewhere between the janitor and the CEO, reasons stop mattering." And That the "Rubicon," he has said, "is crossed when you become a VP."
4. *When behind, leapfrog*: Instead of merely catching up by upgrading the iMac's CD drive, he decided to create an integrated system that would transform the music industry. The result was the combination of iTunes, the iTunes Store, and the iPod, which allowed users to buy, share, manage, store, and play music better than they could with any other devices.
5. *Self-belief*: Jobs's philosophy was that "everything around you that you call life was made up by people that were no smarter than you and you can change it, you can influence it, you can build your own things that other people can use. The people who are crazy enough to think they can change the world are the ones who do."

SWAMI VIVEKANANDA

Swami Vivekananda was a great social reformer and a very inspiring personality who was known in his pre-monastic days as Narendranath Datta. Apart from having a spiritual mind; he was a prolific thinker, great orator, and passionate patriot. He was born in Kolkata on 12 January 1863. He used to practice meditation even from his boyhood, and he was associated with Brahmo Movement for some time.

During his youth, Vivekananda went through a spiritual crisis when he was assailed by doubts about the existence of God. In November 1881, Vivekananda went to meet Sri Ramakrishna who was staying at the Kali Temple in Dakshineshwar. Vivekananda became a frequent visitor to Dakshineshwar, and under the guidance of Sri Ramakrishna he made rapid strides on the spiritual path. In the middle of 1890, Vivekananda left Baranagar Math and embarked on a long journey to explore and discover India. He went on a pilgrimage all over the country, studying the conditions of the people.

Vivekananda was a voracious reader. While he stayed in Chicago, he used to go to the library and borrow large volumes of books and return them to the librarian in a day's time. One day The curious librarian asked Vivekananda why he borrowed books when he did not want to read them, and she was all the more annoyed when he said that he had finished reading all of those books. She said she would take a test and selected a random page from a book and asked him to tell what was written there. Without even a glance at the book he repeated the lines exactly as they were written. She asked him several more questions and he answered all of them without a flaw.

He decided to attend the World Parliament of Religions to spread his message in the West which was scheduled to be held in Chicago in 1893. On the eve of his departure, he adopted the name of Swami Vivekananda. His speeches at the World's Parliament of Religions held in September 1893 made him famous. For 3 years, he spread the Vedanta philosophy and religion in America and England and then returned to India. He founded the Ramakrishna Math and Mission in 1897 and the Belur Math in 1988.

Here is an interesting anecdote. Before going abroad, he was tested by his mother on whether he had the right to preach Hinduism. After a delicious supper, both of them sat down to eat some fruits. Vivekananda cut the fruit and ate it and after that, his mother asked him for the knife; he handed over the knife to his mother and she was more than pleased. She said "you have passed the test and you are now eligible to preach the world," the confused Vivekananda questioned her what was she talking about? His mother replied, "Son, when I asked for the knife, I saw how you handed it to me, you gave the knife by holding its sharp edge and kept the wooden handle of the knife towards me; so that I would not get hurt when I take it and this means you took care of me. And this was your test in which you passed." To have compassion and to be able to take good care of others is a remarkable quality and it is the law of the nature that the more selfless one is the more he/she will receive, and so did Swami Vivekananda.

Vivekananda worked tirelessly towards the betterment of society, in service of the poor and needy, dedicating his entire life for his country and he was one of the key people responsible for the revival of Hindu spiritualism. His message of universal brotherhood and self-awakening remains relevant, especially in the current backdrop of widespread political turmoil around the world.

His leadership attributes as articulated by his biographers are the following:

1. *Believe in yourself*: "Believe in yourself and the world will be at your feet." When one has unwavering faith and belief, he/she finds ways to accomplish things that he/she wants in his/her life. Difficulties, hardships, and struggle make a true leader more determined to succeed.
2. *Dedication to work*: It does not matter what one is doing, but how he/she is doing it makes the ultimate difference. Great opportunities are always possible for the one who is dedicated to what he is doing.
3. *Face the problem – courage*: A true leader will always have a mission and purpose in life. He will be ready to fight the world for it. One cannot solve problems by running away from them. Sooner or later, he/she will need to face the problems and conquer his/her fears.

Here is another interesting anecdote from the life of Swami Vivekananda that illustrates this point. He was about 8 years old when this incident happened. He loved to dangle head down from a tree in his friend's compound. One day he was climbing the tree and an old man approached him and asked him not to climb the tree. The old man was probably scared that the little boy could fall and break his limbs or was just being protective about the Chamapaka flowers on that tree. When the kid questioned him for the reason, the old man told him that there was a ghost living on the tree and it would hurt him and break his neck if he climbed the tree again. The little boy nodded and the old man walked away. The not so convinced 8-year-old boy climbed the tree again. All of his friends were scared and asked him why he was doing it despite knowing that he would be hurt. Swami Vivekananda laughed and said, "What a silly fellow you are! Don't believe everything just because someone tells you! If the old grandfather's story was true then my neck would have been broken long ago," an exceptional common sense of an 8-year-old boy.

4. *Focus on the goal*: "Whatever you are doing, put your whole mind on it. If you are shooting, your mind should only be on the target. Then you will never miss. If you are learning your lessons, think only of the lesson." The difference in quality of two men lies in their ability to concentrate. When one focuses his/her mind, energy, and work towards his/her goals, success is assured. Leaders who work with single pointed focus are better able to achieve their goals and vision.

   Here is another anecdote. While Swami Vivekananda was in America, some boys were standing on the bridge and trying to shoot eggshells that were floating in the water. They failed almost at every try, Vivekananda who was watching them from a distance went close to them, took the gun, and fired 12 times, and every time he fired he hit the eggshell. The inquisitive boys asked him how he did it? He replied "Whatever you are doing, put your whole mind on it. If you are shooting, your mind should be only on the target. Then you will never miss. If you are learning your lessons, think only of the lessons."
5. *Motivator/coach*: Leaders empower their people by believing in them and trusting them, and they rise to greatness as a result. A leader instils belief in others where they can accomplish things that they never thought were possible. Swami Vivekananda preached about the infinite power that resides in each of us and how it unleashes itself to help us achieve anything we want. "All power is within you. You can do anything and everything. Believe in that."
6. *Stay disciplined*: "A leader is one who knows how to obey commands before knowing how to command. Learn obedience first."

DALAI LAMA

His Holiness the 14th Dalai Lama, Tenzin Gyatso, is the spiritual leader of Tibet. The Dalai Lamas are believed to be manifestations of Avalokiteshvara or Chenrezig, the Bodhisattva of Compassion, and the patron saint of Tibet. Bodhisattvas are realized beings inspired by a wish to attain Buddhahood for the benefit of all sentient beings. They have vowed to be reborn in the world to help humanity. In 1950, after China's invasion of Tibet, His Holiness was called upon to assume full political power. In 1954, he went to Beijing and met with Mao Zedong and other Chinese leaders, including Deng Xiaoping and Chou Enlai. Finally, in 1959, following the brutal suppression of the Tibetan national uprising in Lhasa by Chinese troops, His Holiness was forced to escape into exile. Since then, he has been living in Dharamshala in North India.

His Holiness the Dalai Lama is a man of peace. In 1989, he was awarded the Nobel Peace Prize for his non-violent struggle for the liberation of Tibet. He has consistently advocated policies of non-violence, even in the face of extreme aggression. His Holiness has travelled to more than 67 countries spanning

6 continents. He has received over 150 awards, honorary doctorates, prizes, etc., in recognition of his message of peace, non-violence, inter-religious understanding, universal responsibility, and compassion. He has also authored or co-authored more than 110 books.

The Dalai Lama is a very humble man who has always considered himself as a simple Buddhist monk. In his own words, "I feel that is the real me. I feel that the Dalai Lama as a temporal ruler is a man-made institution. As long as the people accept the Dalai Lama, they will accept me. But being a monk is something which belongs to me. No one can change that. Deep down inside, I always consider myself a monk, even in my dreams. So naturally I feel myself as more of a religious person."

The leadership attributes of the Dalai Lama as articulated by his biographers are:

1. *Compassionate*: When one has a genuine care and concern for those he/she leads, there is a greater chance that their welfare can be improved. Be warm-hearted towards others but remember to use logic alongside action. The Dalai Lama believes that when we apply reason, compassion can be extended to all human beings.

   The Dalai Lama in an interview stated that he had three commitments in life. First, on the level of a human being, his commitment is the promotion of human values such as compassion, forgiveness, tolerance, contentment, and self-discipline. In his view, all human beings are the same and all want happiness and do not want suffering. Even people who do not believe in religion recognize the importance of these human values in making their lives happier. He remains committed to talk about the importance of these human values and share them with everyone he meets. Second, on the level of a religious practitioner, his commitment is the promotion of religious harmony and understanding among different religious traditions. Despite philosophical differences, all major world religions have the same potential to create better human beings. It is therefore important for all religious traditions to respect one another and recognize the value of each other's respective traditions. Third, his commitment as a Tibetan who is the Dalai Lama. Tibetans place their trust in him. Therefore, his third commitment is to the Tibetan issue. He has the responsibility to act as free spokesperson of the Tibetans in their struggle for justice. As far as this third commitment, it will cease to exist once a mutually beneficial solution is reached between the Tibetans and Chinese. However, his first two commitments, he mentioned, are lifelong.
2. *Mindful*: A mind affected by fear and anxiety will lead to violence and destructive emotions. One should not fall under the sway of anger or attachment which clouds his/her view when he/she assesses the situations that he/she comes across at home or in the office. When one is mindful, his/her mind is calm – only then will he/she be able to use his/her sense of reason "practically, realistically, and with determination."
3. *Selfless*: Have a generous and cooperative self-interest, rather than a completely selfish one. The Dalai Lama said, "Once you have a genuine sense of concern for others, there's no room for cheating, bullying, or exploitation." A selfless leader will become a great leader, who is honest and transparent in conduct.
4. *Become interconnected*: Buddhists believes in interconnectivity – the idea that people only truly exist in relation with other people. From a Buddhist's perspective, business is a network for these connections, a huge spiritual organism that functions only when all these connections are realized. "The interconnected leader sees himself or herself as the generator of impulses into an interconnected system to realize the purpose of the organization."
5. *Stay positive*: It is no secret that running a business is hard. It is easy for a small business owner or entrepreneur to worry about what could go wrong and prepare for the worst. But, instead, the Dalai Lama encourages a more optimistic approach to business. "Appreciate how rare and full of potential your situation is in this world, then take joy in it, and use it to your best advantage."

A PERSONAL STORY

Let me narrate a personal experience that I had recently. A few friends and I had gone to visit a temple near Bangalore. A saint stayed close by and we went to visit him. Now this saint is from a class called the "Avadhootas." An Avadhoota is someone who has reached the highest level of perfection and does not live by society's norms. They have no desires nor do they live in society as normal humans – they consider themselves one with nature which indeed they are. They consider all living beings including plants, animals, etc. as manifestation of the one pure consciousness and treat everyone equally.

When we reached his small hut (kutir), the Avadhoota (who just had a loin cloth and wore nothing else) was busy cutting vegetables. He motioned for us to sit and then continued to be focused on what he was doing. For the next hour and a half, he continued to cut and make dishes (along with help from an assistant). Not once did he look in our direction nor did he speak with us. So we sat there in silence. A few of us meditated while few others sat, observing the Avdhoota. Meanwhile we were joined by a Swami who was the head of a mutt (ashram) in Karnataka and who was on his way to the Himalayas and wanted to take the blessings of the Avadhoota before he left. He was surprised to see us there and asked us how we knew about the Avadhoota (who was a very low profile person). He told us that the Avadhoota was a very great saint with miraculous powers which he never exhibited. To quote him, he said that this was like having a darshan of "Shiva" himself and that is why he had come there before he left for the Himalayas. After the food was ready, the Avadhoota looked in our direction and asked us whether we would like to have it. Nobody declines such an invitation as it is considered as Prasad (a devotional offering made to God, that is later shared among devotees) from a great soul. We all picked up our plates and had a sumptuous lunch which while being simple was extremely tasty and which we all relished very much.

After we had our lunch (appeared that he had anticipated our arrival and had made it just for us and there was only enough for us), he started talking to us. His message was more by actions than by any talk. He told us that this was his Karma Bhoomi (his place of work) and showed us by his actions the power of focus and concentration even in a simple task such as cooking. That was his message to us that day; do your work with total focus, concentration, and dedication and it does not matter what the nature of work is. But get involved personally, learn the work, and do your best. He then blessed us and let us go.

So, let me summarize the attributes of leadership that we have learnt from the lives of great masters and then try to map it to the 4D's which was first articulated for spiritual life (and is as applicable to material life as well) by the great saint and Philosopher Sri Adi Shankaracharya in his seminal work – *The Tattva Bodha* (An Understanding of the Basic Principles). So this is not something that I take credit for, except that I have tried to classify and map these principles to the leadership attributes as exhibited by the leaders we have studied.

SUMMARY OF LEADERSHIP

Our key take-aways from the analysis of leadership by the study of the few successful leaders are that leadership involves a lifelong commitment to self-mastery, holistic living, and a life of balance. A leader should be able to balance his/her different needs with that of his team and organizational priorities and be the enabling and empowering factor. A great leader is an enabler and a facilitator who helps to build teams with a shared vision and provide them with space, opportunity, and an environment for creativity and growth. Team members are selected for their attitude and trained to hone their skills. Learning and growth take place both of the leader and the team and together they contribute to the progress of the enterprise.

Leader	Leadership attribute	Leadership principle
Mahatma Gandhi	A shared vision	Desire and determination
	Strength of character	Self-discipline
	Faith in oneself	Desire and determination
	Self-mastery and control of mind	Self-discipline
	Self-discipline	Discipline
	Health	Discrimination and discipline
Nelson Mandela	Be brave and courageous	Self-discipline
	Persistence	Desire and determination
	Spread happiness through your team	Discriminating mind
	Lead from behind	Discriminating mind
	Focus on converting the enemy into a frenemy	Discriminating mind
Bill Gates	Focus on the goal	Dispassion
	Believe in the power of your dreams – passion	Desire and determination
	Take risks	Discriminating mind
	Creativity	Discriminating mind
	Caring	Self-discipline
Steve Jobs	Simplicity	Self-discipline
	Focus	Dispassion
	Take responsibility end to end	Discriminating mind
	When behind, leapfrog	Creative self-disciplined mind
	Self-belief	Desire and determination, self-discipline
Swami Vivekananda	Believe in yourself	Self-discipline
	Dedication to work	Dispassion
	Face the problem, courage	Determination and discriminating mind
	Focus on the goal	Dispassion
	Motivator/coach	Discriminating mind, self-discipline
	Stay disciplined	Self-discipline
Dalai Lama	Stay interconnected, stay positive	Self-discipline
	Compassionate	Self-discipline
	Mindful	Dispassion, discrimination
	Selfless	Self-discipline
	Become interconnected	Dispassion
	Stay positive	Self-discipline
Other skills	Managing uncertainty	Discriminating mind
	Continuous learning	Desire
	Committed to personal growth	Desire
	Empathy for colleagues	Discriminating mind
	Committed to colleagues growth	Discriminating mind
	Create a conducive positive energizing space	Discriminating mind

In organizations, leaders are most often recognized for achieving external results – revenue, profit, new product breakthroughs, cost savings, market share, etc. Of course, this a necessity in an organizational context but one must also reflect on how these could be achieved and improved upon. What is it that is required? Where do the external results come from? Is focusing on external achievement the sole source of greater accomplishment? Could it be that our single-minded focus on external results is causing us to miss the underlying dynamics supporting sustainable peak performance? Are we missing out on peak performance by not focusing on the individuals and the traits required to make this all happen?

4Ds

To summarize, the major leadership principles that need to be studied:

1. ***Discrimination*** (Viveka in Sanskrit) is basically using the intellect to control the emotional mind. In the Tattva Bodha, it is used in a spiritual sense, i.e. the differentiation between the real and the unreal, between the permanent and the impermanent. The firm knowledge of what is ephemeral and what is eternal is called one's discriminative ability. This is as true in material life as in spiritual life. In a leadership context, it is the ability to discriminate between the superficial and the underlying reason/cause by applying logic and using the intellect, rather than reacting emotionally to every single stimulus/event.
2. ***Dispassion.*** From discrimination follows dispassion (also known as Vairagya in Sanskrit). In the spiritual sense, dispassion is the non-craving and/or non-attachment to objects of sensory pleasure. It is disinterested detachment towards all the pleasures and objects of this world. It gives great mental strength as the focus is turned towards action and not the results. This leads to better quality of action and its implementation with full vigour. The mind is not constrained by worry about the results. This is extremely important in a leadership (and life) context too, where once a course of action has been decided the focus needs to be on its implementation not constrained by a worry on the results. Many leaders have pointed out to this being a very important principle, to be dispassionate – to basically focus on the action and not be too worried on the results.
3. ***Discipline.*** Inner strengths that almost all leaders we studied have said are important.

   > If you suffer it is because of you, and if you feel blissful it is because of you. Nobody else is responsible – only you and you alone.
   >
   > – Osho

   These are

   - *Mind control* (Sama in Sanskrit). We will study the mind in detail in one of the later chapters but simply put "mind is nothing but thought forms" (Ramana Maharishi). So mind control is basically thought control, which of course is easier said than done. The purity of the thoughts can be maintained by good practices such as concentration, meditation, prayer, and music. A mind not under the control of the intellect is dangerous as is the case with many managers and leaders who have exhibited the extraordinary warped nature of their minds being self-centred, selfish, and brutal. Mind control goes hand in hand with exercising a discriminating mind and exercising sense control.
   - *Sense control* (Dama in Sanskrit). The sense organs determine what stimulus enter the mind and are like the gateways of the mind to the outer world. By nature, the senses run after sense objects without any discrimination. It is only by applying one's intellect and applying logic and reasoning that they can be kept in check. The Kathopanishad compares sense organs to horses, sensory objects to the path it traverses on, mind to the reins, and the intellect to the charioteer. Neither the reins nor the horses should be allowed to determine the direction of the chariot. Only the charioteer should. Similarly, a leader needs to have his/her mind and senses under the control of the intellect.

- *Withdrawal of senses* (called Uparama in Sanskrit). It is achieved through reduction of extrovert activities and turning the mind away from sensual objects and from worldly longings. This comes naturally when one practices mind and sense control along with discrimination and using the intellect. In a leadership context, this leads to focus and persistence and not being distracted by issues and matters that are not core to one's objectives.
- *Forbearance* (called Tithiksha in Sanskrit). Forbearance is the ability to bear without reacting, complaining, or blaming oneself or others for negative results and/or experiences either at the physical, emotional, or intellectual level. It is the tolerance of conditions outside one's control, natural, social, or physical without losing one's coolness. This gives one a tension-free calm mind that is suitable for reflection, and as seen in our analysis of leadership traits this is a vital leadership quality.
- *Faith or conviction* (called Sraddha in Sanskrit). In a leadership context, it refers to a firm self-belief based on an open, alert mind and work with determination towards the chosen goal to realize it.
- *Single-pointedness of mind* (Samadhana in Sanskrit). This is the ability to have the goal in one's sights always and be constantly focused in one's efforts to reach it. Developing concentration power is the key and we will therefore explore "concentration" in greater detail.

4. ***Desire and determination*** (Mumukshutvam in Sanskrit). Intense desire. In a leadership sense, there must be a purpose (which has deep personal meaning and which is larger than the leader), something that strikes a chord in the people who follow/form the team, and which is aligned to deeply held values. Having once decided on the purpose, a deep desire (meant in a positive way) that coupled with determination and persistence is the hallmark of a true leader. The intensity of purpose enables the leader to both influence his team and followers and also imbibe all other qualities needed for success/achievement of the purpose.

KEY TAKEAWAY

This chapter examined some enduring leadership principles based on the lives of some of the acknowledged great leaders. We then classified these leadership principles into four main buckets: dispassion, discrimination, self-discipline, and desire and determination (defining purpose and following it through). These leadership principles were defined and explained in terms of real-life examples and how they helped in success in life and leadership. These principles are also applicable to all: a student, a housewife, an entrepreneur, a businessman, an executive, a politician, and others. The following few chapters will dig deeper into some of these leadership themes and in order to do so we will begin with understanding our self a little better – what are we constituted of and what exactly is this mind that we seek to keep a check on.

3 The Building Blocks – Understanding the Self

According to the Upanishads (the fountainhead of Indian spirituality), consciousness or awareness is an independent entity that makes the body sentient. The body is nothing but a bundle of matter and may be sentient or not. What makes it sentient is the presence of consciousness that makes the body capable of feeling/seeing/understanding the surroundings and distinguishes it from any inert object, for example a car or a cycle. The body is also made of chemicals. But this bundle of chemicals is different from a table or any other inert object that is also made up of chemicals. In a human body, it is referred to as biochemistry because this bundle of body is alive and sentient and whatever makes this body alive and sentient is called consciousness. The body (primarily the mind) is nothing but a reflecting medium (I must acknowledge Sri Swami Paramarthananda, my Vedic Guru, who has taught me the Upanishads and this chapter has been shaped by the wisdom that I have imbibed from him as also some of the examples that he often quotes).

It is important for us to understand the nature of this consciousness because the entire premise is that the body and the mind are evolutes of this consciousness. If we need to keep the body and the mind fit, active, and under control, it is very necessary to understand the nature of this consciousness and its relationship to our mind and body. This approach is totally divergent to Western material thought that consciousness is a property of the physical body, the resultant of the brain and its wiring (the firing of the neurons), and an outcome of the resultant chemical processes. While science has started to veer away from this thought (very initial stages and especially so in quantum physics), it still considers consciousness to be the result of various biochemical processes. The corollary of Western thought is that since consciousness is a property of the body, life can be recreated in a laboratory which so far has not been successful (except for some unverified and unsustained claims). The corollary of Vedic thought is that this whole universe is one consciousness and hence interconnected even though we appear in several different types of physical bodies. This is an elevating thought, which once internalized has a deep positive bearing on thought and action.

If we understand and experience that we are the reflections of that one consciousness, this will have a bearing on our physical, mental, and psychological well-being.

Almost all processes can be controlled to some extent by conscious thought and bringing awareness to what we do and feel.

This goes for biochemical processes in the body as well, which is what science is now finding out. Some of the findings are presented in the next few chapters.

CHARACTERISTICS OF CONSCIOUSNESS

There is a story of King Janaka who was a great king, never defeated in war, who once got a nightmare that he was so badly defeated and exiled out of his own kingdom and that he could not even get a bowl of gruel to eat. After walking for many hours, with hunger, thirst and fatigue, he encountered a kind-hearted soul who finally gave him a bowl of rice. As he was going to sip the gruel, a hawk swooped down and knocked the food into the dust.

King Janaka sat up in bed screaming. His royal courtiers came running and asked him what the matter was? King Janaka kept repeating "Is this the reality, or is that the reality?" No amount of soothing from anyone helped. Finally, a great spiritual master came, listened to King Janaka, and gave him spiritual enlightenment, the gist of which is as follows. The spiritual master asked Janaka, "Did you *experience* what happened in the dream?" Janaka responded affirmatively. The spiritual master asked, "Are you *experiencing* your present waking state?" Again, Janaka said "yes." The spiritual master then said, "Neither that is the reality, nor this is the reality." Janaka was stunned. The spiritual master continued, "Only you are the reality." The "you" in the answer refers to the "atman," that is the soul, consciousness, or witness. The Mandukya Upanishad says that every person experiences three states – the "waker" (waking state), the dreamer (dreaming state), and the sleeper (deep sleep or total unawareness) state. As a waker, one experiences with his/her body (senses) and mind; as a dreamer, one experiences with his/her mind; and as a sleeper, one experiences nothing. But one's soul or consciousness is neither the "waker" nor the dreamer or the sleeper. One's true or real nature is none of those three but his/her consciousness. This is the answer to the deep philosophical and spiritual question "Who am I?" I am not my body, nor mind, nor ego. I am my consciousness. Consciousness pervades my body and mind, and pervades all my three states mentioned earlier; yet consciousness is separated from them, and it is the only reality. It is the only eternal, immanent entity which is one with nature and the universe.

So, how can I know or understand consciousness? Swami Vivekananda said, "The one who goes to the mountain top seeking the answer is lost; the one who is immersed in the mundane material world or ego is lost." The only way is to live a wholesome life – a life of virtue, values, grace, goodness, and compassion.

First, consciousness is not a part, product, property of this body. According to the Upanishads, unlike the height, weight, complexion, etc. which are the properties of the body, sentiency or consciousness is not the property of the body nor is it a part of the body such as the hair, nail, and skin which are all parts of the body. If this statement is true, we can no more state that life or consciousness is generated in the body or the brain. It is not a similar process to enzymes being produced in the body or as blood that is manufactured in the body and cells created in the body. Consciousness is not even a product generated by the material brain. The body cannot generate life by itself, very unlike what the pharaohs believed, which is why they preserved their bodies as mummies. In summary, life is not a product of matter. So the first characteristic is that consciousness is not a part, property, or a product of the body. The body or its part can only reflect consciousness, according to Vedic thought, much as a light bulb can reflect electricity. To understand the truth of this statement requires a deep dive into meditation, observing the mind and being a silent witness.

The second characteristic is that consciousness is an invisible independent entity that pervades the body and makes the body sentient and alive. A similar example will be the electricity that makes the fan active. A fan cannot run without electricity as the driving force. This invisible electricity is a separate independent principle/force and is neither a property of the fan nor a part of the fan nor even a product of the fan. Electricity exists independent of the fan much like consciousness is to the body. All our bodies can be compared with the fans or the bulbs that operate due to the driving force of the electricity. Similarly, this inert bundle of matter called our body is alive and kicking due to its invisible principle called consciousness. The moment when consciousness departs, this body decays as all the subprocesses fall apart. So the consciousness is an invisible and independent entity that pervades the body and makes it alive.

This invisible independent consciousness is not limited or circumscribed by or confined to the boundaries of the body. It also extends beyond the body, just as the electricity is not confined to the boundaries of the fan. Consciousness is boundless, limitless, dimension less (no height, no width, no length), and it is beyond all these. All these belong to the realm of the physical body, just as the length belongs to the blades of the fan and not to the electricity. So the third characteristic is that consciousness has no boundaries. It is all pervading and is not constrained by space.

This invisible, independent consciousness will continue to survive even after the body medium dies, perishes, or is destroyed. Just as, even after the destruction of the bulb and the light, even after the destruction of the fan and its rotation, the electricity continues to be present in the circuit. Similarly even after the body dies, the consciousness continues to exist. It is, therefore, a permanent principle – an eternal principle. Invisible consciousness is not therefore limited by time. Hence, consciousness does not have space and time limitations.

In the Bhagavad Gita, it is mentioned that "the soul is never born, nor does it ever die; nor does it become a soul after being born. For, it is unborn, eternal, everlasting and primeval; even though the body is slain, the soul is not." This is very close to what quantum physicists are currently saying.

After death, the surviving consciousness cannot be contacted or recognized by us, not because it is not present but because the medium of the body no longer exists. The surviving consciousness after the fall of the body is unrecognizable. The principle is similar to the examples of bulb and fan given earlier. We recognize the electricity only through the gadgets such as bulb and fan. If they break down, we cannot recognize the electricity even though it is always present. It is just a driving force and the end instrument which it operates does not matter to it.

The unified field theory that physicists talk about points in the same direction – that the entire creation is one composite whole and all of life, whether animate or inanimate, manifest or unmanifest, is intimately connected. In other words, whatever one thinks, feels, says, or does spreads like ripples into unending space, mixing, merging, and colliding with other ripples and causing new ripples. This is a very dynamic idea, which lends universality to each and every human being and gives life status and importance that extend far beyond ones imagination and expectation. The yogis have discovered through contemplation and certain inner processes that this gross body has evolved from pure consciousness, that is neither bound by time nor by space and is spread throughout the universe. Hence it is important to understand this physical body on how matter and energy which comprise this body have evolved from consciousness and how they will merge back into consciousness. Once one has a basic understanding of the evolutes of consciousness (called tattva or principles in Sanskrit), it is possible to exert some measures of control over it through processes such as focusing awareness, mindfulness, and meditation. This also helps us gain a better purpose in life and of freeing ourselves from unnecessary stress and phobias. As the Tantric says, "where Consciousness goes, energy flows and where energy grows, Consciousness glows."

Let me illustrate this with a beautiful story.

A king in Japan sent his son to a mystic, to a master, to learn awareness. The king was old. He said to the son, "Put your total energy into it because unless you are aware, you are not going to succeed me. I will not give this kingdom to a man who is asleep and unconscious. It is not a question of father and son. My father had given it to me only when I attained awareness. I was not the right person, because I was not his eldest son, I was his youngest son. But my other two brothers, who were older than me, could not attain it."

"The same is going to happen to you. And the problem is even more complicated because I have only one son: if you do not attain awareness, the kingdom is going into somebody else's hands. You will be a beggar on the streets. So it is a question of life and death for you. Go to this man; he has been my master. Now he is very old, but I know that if anybody can teach you, he is the one. Tell him, 'My father is sick, old, can die any day. Time is short, and I have to become fully aware before he dies; otherwise I lose the kingdom.'"

A very symbolic story too: "If you are not aware, you lose the kingdom."

The king's son went to the old master in the mountains. He said to the master, "I have been sent by your disciple, the king." The master was very old, older than his father. He said, "I remember that man. He was really an authentic seeker. I hope you will prove to be of the same quality, of the same genius, of the same totality, of the same intensity." The young prince said, "I will do everything." The master said, "Then start cleaning in the commune. And remember one thing – that I will be hitting you at any time. You may be cleaning the floor and I may come from the back and hit you with my stick, so be alert."

He said, "But I have come to learn about awareness ..."

The master said, "This is how you will learn."

One year passed. In the beginning he was getting so many hits every day, but slowly he started becoming aware. Even the footsteps of the old man and (he would have been doing anything – howsoever absorbed in the work), he would become immediately aware that the master was around. The prince would be ready. After 1 year, the master tried to hit him from the back while he was deeply involved in talking with another inmate of the ashram. The prince continued talking, but still caught hold of the stick before the stick could reach his body.

The master said, "That's right. Now this is the end of the first lesson. The second lesson begins tonight."

The prince said, "I used to think that this was all. This is only the first lesson? How many lessons are there?" The old man said, "It depends on you. The second lesson is that now I will be hitting you while you are asleep, and you have to be alert in your sleep." The prince said, "My God. How can one be alert in sleep?" The old man said, "Don't be worried. Thousands of my disciples have passed through the test. Your father has passed through the test. It is not impossible. It is difficult, but it is a challenge."

From that night he was getting hits 6 times, 8 times, 12 times in the night. Sleep was difficult. But within 6 months he started feeling a certain awareness inside himself. And one day when the master was just going to hit him, with closed eyes he said – "Don't bother. You are too old. It hurts me; you are taking so much trouble. I am young, I can survive these hits."

The master said, "You are blessed. You have passed the second lesson. But up to now I have been hitting with my wooden staff. The third lesson is that now I will start hitting, from tomorrow morning, with a real sword. Be alert! Just a moment of unconsciousness and you are finished." Early in the morning the master used to sit in the garden, just listening to the birds singing, the flowers opening, and the sun rising. The prince thought, "Now it is becoming dangerous! A wooden stick was hard, difficult, but it was not going to kill me. A real sword ..." He was a swordsman but he was not given any chance to protect himself, and only awareness was going to be his protection.

An idea came to his mind: "This old man is really dangerous. Before he starts his third lesson, I would like to check whether he himself can pass the third test or not. If he is putting my life at risk, I cannot allow him to do it without checking whether he is worthy of it or not." And these were only thoughts that he was thinking lying down in his bed, and it was a cold morning.

And the master said, "Come out of your blanket, you idiot! Do you want to hit your own master with a sword? Feel ashamed! I can hear the footsteps of your thoughts ... drop the idea." He had heard. Nothing was said to him, nothing was done to him.

Thoughts are also things or objects. Thoughts also, while moving, make sounds, and those who are fully alert can read one's thoughts. The prince was really ashamed. He fell at the feet of the master and he said, "Please forgive me. I am really stupid."

Since it was a question of a sword, a real sword, he became aware of everything around him, even his own breathing and his heartbeat. He started becoming aware of a zephyr passing through the leaves and even the slightest movement like that of a dead leaf stirring in the wind, he was aware. The master tried a few times but found him always ready. He could not hit him with the sword because he could not find him unconscious or unmindful. He was just alert. It was a question of death – one cannot afford to be anything but alert.

After 3 days, the master could not find a single moment or a single loophole. After the third day, he called him and told him, "Now you can go and tell your father – and this is the letter from me – that the kingdom is yours."

Awareness is a process of being more and more awake. What this implies is that the first step is to appreciate that awareness or consciousness and the mind are two separate things. The second step is to ensure that the mind does not wander and that our awareness moves within the mind. If one's awareness is scattered through the mind all day, then one's energy is also flowing all over the place. For most this happens as a matter of habit. Success (both material and spiritual) is a manifestation of where and how focused this energy is directed at. Success also depends on how much emotion we can bring into what we do. As my Guru Avadhoot Shivananda said "Emotion is energy in motion." The more positive emotion one brings into one's life, the more energy is generated and the focus helps channelize this into proper use. On the other hand, negative emotions, such as anger, hate, addictions, greed, and jealousy, can work in the opposite manner and all one's energy is consumed and depleted by these negative emotions. When one can concentrate on his/her awareness towards one or a few things, he/she begins to direct his/her energy towards it, and that object of desire starts to manifest in one's life. The two key requirements are "positive emotions" and "focus." It would also be useful to understand emotions, energy, and awareness a little better – where do they arise from them, how do they manifest, and how can one control them. Since we know from science that energy and matter are interconvertible, and that energy is subtle matter, a better understanding and control of energy will help us control our bodies and minds better. Mind is also subtle matter and the subtler it is, the more powerful the medium.

The Upanishads consider mind as the subtle form of matter, and the body and its components are considered the grossest forms. Consciousness, on the other hand, is considered finer than "mind matter" and is considered all pervasive, omnipresent, and omniscient.

Swami Vivekananda explained the mind–body relationship from his own transcendental experience: "The body is just the external crust of the mind. They are not two different things; they are just as the oyster and its shell, they are but two aspects of one thing; the internal substance of the oyster takes up matter from outside, and manufactures the shell. In the same way, the internal fine force which is called mind takes up gross matter from outside, and from that manufactures this external shell, the body. Hence, the mind is connected with the body which is why when the mind is disturbed, the body also becomes disturbed. Consciousness or awareness on the other hand can be constant and undisturbed and for the practiced meditator a completely independent entity, the witness, which observes the thoughts or no-thoughts of the mind." The world that we create for ourselves is the external manifestation of our mind. There is no world without our minds and hence the imperative to understand and control the emotions that run through the mind. The better the mind stuff the better and more peaceful our lives. This is why many people are perfectly happy and contended with very little material stuff; they have created and defined their world differently and in a way that is appealing to them.

THE FIVE BODIES

Modern science has been able to understand and study in great detail all the physical processes and actions/ reactions of the physical body including how the brain functions, the release of biochemicals and their impact on the body, and to some extent the mind, the rise of diseases, and their treatment. However, it still has little or no understanding of what enables all these activities. For example, a dead body almost has all the physical organs but there is no process (other than decay that is happening in that body). Science explains the "how" very well (at least the visible material part) but it still has a long way to go explain the "why." Here scriptures and one's own meditation and experience help. There is something else (call it consciousness or awareness) that drives the body towards what it does and it is this that tantra, yoga, and spirituality deals with, in great detail. This has nothing to do with religion but is a result of deep focus and concentration on one's internal process where other faculties like intuition open up. Obviously, science has reservations but let us keep in mind that science had reservations on a number of things that it could not prove until new instruments to study such phenomenon were invented and then long-held positions were reversed, for example the movement of the earth around the sun and the impact of yoga and mindfulness on the body all of which science had decried earlier. The proof of the pudding is in the eating so if there is a better system that enables one to be healthier, more focused, happy, and productive in an organizational context, such a system should be adopted. Science can then research and validate or invalidate the same based on facts and findings.

Here is a beautiful story that explains this very simply.

Thousands of years ago, in a beautiful hermitage in the middle of a forest lived a learned Guru. Among his many talented disciples, perhaps the most talented was his own son though the Guru showed him no special favours. One day the boy respectfully approached his master. When he was granted permission to ask a question, he reverently asked, "What is God?"

The Guru replied, "God is food." Then he was silent.

The boy correctly surmised this to mean that he must study not only food but also what the food creates – the human body. Many years passed as his observation deepened, and at last he concluded that there was something more powerful than the physical body nourished by food or the *Annamaya Kosha.*

Once again, he approached his master and asked, "What is God?"

This time the sage replied, "Prana (the life force or the breath) is God (Brahman)."

The boy plunged this time into an intense study of prana, mastering the techniques of controlling the life force energy through pranayama and related disciplines. But some years later, he realized that there is something else that governs the energy through breath or the *Pranamaya Kosha.* Once again, he went to his master and reverently repeated his query, "What is God?"

"God is mind," the Guru intoned and sank once again into the depths of his meditative bliss.

The disciple then did not waste a moment and plunged into a deep state of meditation.

He realized that there is something subtler than the mind or the *Manomaya Kosha.* So, he prepared himself once more to receive the best that the master had to offer. He once again asked, "What is God?" "God is intelligence." This was the next message he received from the Guru.

By this time, he was able to plunge into the depths of intuitive perception. He began to unravel the mysteries of *Vijnanyanmaya Kosha,* which is the basis of Indian spiritual wisdom for centuries. But there was still another step to take; and once more he asked his master, this time with the confidence of a true seeker, "What is God?"

With a satisfied smile and infinite love, the master replied with an air of finality, "Bliss is God!" When the ripened seeker delved into the *Anandamaya Kosha,* it gave him the sheer experience of bliss. He dissolved in it totally. The ecstasy of divine realization became his very being and he was enlightened.

The spiritual path is an experiential one – subtle and beautiful – in contrast to dry theories and rhetoric. Just like the talented seeker in the story, one must have a combination of many things such as patience, discipline, intuition, wisdom, and devotion to attain anything in life.

The story gives insight into the *Pancha Kosha* (five sheaths or layers) that make a human being. They are:

- *Annamaya Kosha* or the food sheath
- *Pranamaya Kosha* or the breath sheath
- *Manomaya Kosha* or the mind sheath
- *Vijgyanamaya Kosha* or the intellect sheath
- *Anandamaya Kosha* or the bliss sheath.

Often, we identify ourselves with one of these layers. We either think of ourselves as just the body, thoughts, or emotions and this limited identification is what makes us miserable. The result is that we suffer when the body is in pain or when our emotions are in turmoil. This leaves us with the question – how do we expand our identification and realize our blissful self? Taking a clue from the protagonist of our story, one answer is to attend to the five sheaths.

As mentioned earlier, every living being is comprised of five bodies or sheaths, each more subtle than the previous one. This finds its ultimate expression in a human body, but plants and animals also have these bodies to some degree. It is important to understand these bodies since some of the exercises/activities that are suggested later on, presume a basic understanding of these bodies and are interventions at the subtle level. The five bodies and their functions are

Gross Body (Food Sheath)

This is made up of the food we eat. This body is constituted of the physical organs of action (hands, feet, etc.), physical organs of knowledge (ears, eyes, etc.), and the various body parts including the brain and the central nervous system – all gross in nature. We interact with the physical world primarily through the gross body since the physical universe is also gross matter. Modern medical science treats almost all physical ailments at this level, which is why the success of such treatment is good on the physical/symptomatic level but without any guarantee of non-recurrence since the roots of the illnesses are at the mental level (the mind) which is not in the gross body. Hence the genesis of the problem remains. This is why yoga and many other systems place great emphasis on the food one consumes. They have a bearing on health as we will discuss in detail later. "You are what you eat" is a popular saying.

Physical Body

The physical body consists of 20 components (principles) and are listed as follows:

- Five organs of action
- Five organs of knowledge
- Five sense perceptions
- Five elementals.

Organs of Action (Output)

The organs of action are basically

- Hands
- Feet
- Mouth
- Genitals
- Anus.

Organs of Knowledge (Input)

The organs of knowledge act as the stimulus to the mind which then results in action through the organs of action. They are listed as follows:

- Ears
- Skin
- Eyes
- Tongue
- Nose.

What is referred to as organs of knowledge are not the external organs per se (which are found even in a dead body) but the invisible power behind the external organs which makes these organs function properly.

Five Elements

The five elementals that are parts of the physical body are:

1. Space
2. Air
3. Fire
4. Water
5. Earth.

Five Sense Perceptions

The five sense perceptions at the physical level are:

1. Hearing
2. Touch
3. Sight
4. Taste
5. Smell.

The gross physical body similar to the subtle mind (which is also subtle matter) is comprised of different proportions of the basic elements and this determines their grossness and subtleness.

The food sheath or the gross body is basically inert matter and will not operate without some external force that pervades it and makes it function. In addition, this gross body that is formed from the food we eat takes on the hue of the food consumed, which is why we need to be very careful of what we consume.

The physical body as we all know can be maintained with

- *Healthy diet* – Balanced natural diet of seasonal fruits and vegetables, available naturally and without being refrigerated. Traditionally, food in India is consumed within 3–4 hours of its cooking and is not refrigerated as it loses its "prana." Prana is the invisible "energy" that drives all activities and can be obtained from food and also through the air we breathe.
- *Healthy regimen* – Exercises such as yoga, pilates, Pilates walking/running, and aerobics.
- *Proper breathing* – Extremely important as this is one of the most important sources of prana. This also strengthens immunity by strengthening the respiratory system. Pranayama or the control of prana is the fourth part of the eightfold yoga system. Prana is acquired and retained by controlling the breath. This is a whole branch of study and one can increase the heat and cold in the body by changing the way one breathes. Many diseases can also be healed by proper breathing. There are many studies that have currently been conducted to understand the effects of pranayama which are well documented.
- *Use of herbs* – Ayurveda (science of long life) is one of the oldest Indian systems of medicines. Primarily various herbal concoctions are used to balance the three humours (otherwise called vata (the energy of movement), pita (the energy of digestion or metabolism), and kapha (the energy that forms the body structure) in the body. This system deals with ensuring long life by treating the root cause and not the symptoms of the disease and is done mainly through the use of herbs. Commonly used herbs that are also called wonder drugs are ginger, pepper, turmeric, and spices such as cinnamon.

The Prana Body (The Energy Sheath or Body of Physiological Processes)

No physical activity is possible without energy. Energy is obtained from the food we eat, the air we breathe, and most importantly from our thoughts, which is why constant worry and negative emotions such as hatred and anger deplete one's energy more than hard physical labour. Conversely good positive thoughts and self-awareness can supplement the body and mind with more prana. This is the basis of healing systems such as pranic healing. The pranic energy drives all the physiological processes such as respiration, digestion, circulation, excretion, and reproduction.

Here is a story from the Prashnopanishad that illustrates the importance of prana.

Prana is the energy of creation of all life. In this version of the short story from the Prashnopanishad, we get an insightful introduction to the importance of the vital energy.

Once upon a time, looking everywhere, traveling far and wide, were six seekers of truth and wisdom. After many miles and long journeys, they heard of a great sage who, they believed, would be able to help them in their quest. They arrived at a hermitage that was deep in the forest. The sage asked them to spend a year with him. The seekers agreed and became the sage's disciples. After a year, one of them asked the sage, "Which sense is of the greatest importance in sustaining the body?" The sage answered them with this story.

Once upon a time, there were five senses: hearing, sight, smell, taste, and touch. One day as they were sitting around, they talked about all the things they could do. The senses were somewhat boastful about their abilities and importance and they claimed to be the rulers of the body. They claimed, "Look at us, for we are remarkably special." They boasted, "There is no way the body can survive without us."

Each sense, in turn, showed off its abilities. Hearing filled the space with music that breathed emotion and passion which stirred the soul. Sight matched the music with a breath-taking splendour of swirling, magical forms in exquisite shades of colours. Smell, in a puff of breath, perfumed the expanse with heavenly aromas. Taste, not to be outdone, exhaled out a cornucopia of mouth-watering flavours. Touch made the whole body vibrant with each and every breath, tingling with soft warmth and delicious coolness. They all lavished praise for one other. It was quite a show.

Prana quietly breathed in and out, watching this awesome spectacle. It was present simply there. With the in-breath, it observed the senses; with the out-breath, it observed the senses. After letting the senses go on for a while, prana said, "None of you reigns supreme in the body." No one was listening. The senses had no time or awareness of anything else. They were completely blind to everything beyond themselves and certainly had no sight of prana. Prana tried again. The senses, in their total self-absorption, had no attention to spare for prana. Prana left angrily.

As prana left, the sounds, colours, fragrances, tastes, physical sensations, and the mind, all faded and disappeared. The senses ceased to exist. The senses had no idea of what had happened. As prana returned, they found themselves and knew that they were subservient to prana as they were no longer there when prana had left. The senses were suddenly vulnerable and scared.

Prana reappeared and suddenly they were aware of prana. Similar to a light switch, they were turned on and off by this vital energy over which they had no control, but the energy had total control over them. With this awareness came the instant realization that they existed because of prana and that this vital energy was far more powerful than them. They did not rule the body at all in any way. Prana did.

As they bowed down in respect, prana told them, "Dividing myself five times and spreading out in the body, I change my form and create the Senses from myself and thus give life in the body."

Prana in this story is mahaprana and the five sub-pranas in this story are *apana*, *prana*, *samana*, *udana*, and *vyana* which are explained later.

What do we instinctively do when there is a terrible smell? Hold the breath – no breath, no smell. When something tastes terrible, hold the breath! No breath, no taste. When we need to lift a heavy object, what do we do – hold the breath.

The senses and the mind are born from prana, are a manifestation of prana, and return to be absorbed into prana. In fact, the senses and the mind are absorbed into prana every night during the phase of deep sleep. Deep sleep is so important to all of us. Without a withdrawal from the unceasing activity of the senses and the mind, we feel exhausted and depleted of vitality. If we have a restless night with lots of dreams, the sleep is not refreshing but tiring. Deep sleep is refreshing and invigorating. However, we are not aware during deep sleep.

Although it is possible to withdraw awareness from the constant chatter of the senses and the mind through meditation, just be aware of prana and experience the same relaxation as deep sleep, while being fully aware of it. If we listen carefully, we hear the notes of the music of the breath of life, prana.

All breathing exercises are an attempt to recharge the "prana" (loosely defined as energy) in the body through the process of inhalation and exhalation deeply and with mindfulness. It is important to have an understanding of this body as even a simple awareness and mindfulness of this body get far greater results and have greater impact on the mind than pure physical exercises. In fact, asanas (popularly known as yoga) is not just physical postures but a combination of mindful awareness of the physical action and aligning the breath to the posture. This will have a great beneficial impact both on the physical body (reducing illnesses or recovering from them speedily) and also on reducing and eliminating issues of the mind (worry, stress, tension, etc.) as the prana is the bridge between the physical body and the mind. Furthermore, it is this pranic energy that helps to maintain a calm and peaceful mind which is so essential for the knowledge worker.

This is subtler than the gross physical body and not visible to the naked eye which instead of food is made of prana or energy. One's body is enveloped by this field of prana which follows the physical body.

What is Prana or Energy?

Prana is the "life force" or the "vital principle" that causes this body to act and is similar to any machine that can move or work only if it has energy. A good example is an automobile. We fill it with petrol and this petrol is converted into energy that enables the car to move. Our physical body also moves, and this movement requires energy that in turn needs a fuel tank, which in the case of a human is the stomach. Our fuel tank, which we constantly replenish with food, is the stomach and the intake of food gets converted into energy or life – force. This internal energy is called prana.

There are five principle pranas (there are many sub-pranas but I will not elaborate on those). These fivefold pranic or physiological functions are:

1. Respiratory system (externally breathed in is "prana" air)
2. Excretory system ("apana" air)
3. Circulatory system ("vyana" air)
4. Digestive system ("samana" air)
5. Emergency system ("udana" air), which is an emergency system for the body and used only rarely and is used to protect and save our body and health. This power gets activated whenever any poison or toxin, which is a threat to our health, enters our body and manifests either in the form of vomiting or purging until the poison is thrown out.

It is important to have an understanding of this body energy since some extent of understanding and control of energy makes one physically, mentally, emotionally, and spiritually a healthy person.

The prana is divided into five main types:

1. *Prana* is situated in the head, centred in the middle of the forehead, and its energy pervades the chest region. The flow of prana is inwards and upwards. It nourishes the brain and the eyes and governs reception of all things: food, air, senses, and thoughts. This is the fundamental energy in the body and directs and feeds into the four other pranas.
2. *Apana* is situated in the pelvic floor and its energy pervades the lower abdomen. The flow of apana is downwards and outwards and its energy nourishes the organs of digestion, reproduction, and elimination. Apana governs the elimination of all substances from the body: carbon monoxide, urine, stool, etc.
3. *Vyana* is situated in the heart and lungs and flows throughout the entire body. The flow of vyana moves from the centre of the body to the periphery. It governs circulation of all substances throughout the body and assists the other pranas with their functions.
4. *Samana* is situated in the abdomen with its energy centred in the navel. The flow of samana is from the periphery of the body to the centre. It governs the digestion and assimilation of all substances: food, air, experiences, emotions, and thoughts.
5. *Udana* is situated in the throat and it has a circular flow around the neck and head. It functions to "hold us up" and governs speech, self-expression, and growth. This gets activated and reverses all functions at the time of disease (e.g. vomiting if one has ingested something that is poisonous to the system) and more particularly in death.

One can control and cultivate these energies by simply bringing one's focus and awareness to them. Through this conscious control and cultivation, one can also improve one's health and well-being to ensure a calm and peaceful mind. The prana is the bridge between the body and the mind as it is all but impossible to control the mind directly. The prana through the breath is the means to control the mind which is why almost all practices to control the mind start with breathing practices. In Hindu mythology (as also in worship which is nothing but an externalization of an internal process), Hanuman the popular monkey God is nothing but the mind (the mind is very often compared with a monkey since that is its nature and is hence symbolized as such) and the father of Hanuman is supposed to be the wind God, otherwise symbolized as the breath. So in a sense it is the breath that gives rise to the mind (the wind gives rise to the monkey mind) and similarly the only way to control the mind is to control the wind or the air one breathes and through it the prana or energy that feeds the mind. Every single God can be explained in terms of symbolisms used which was the way it was made popular to the masses in a way that was easily understood. Once one has faith and devotion through external worship it can then be easily internalized.

While the blood in the physical body moves through the blood vessels namely arteries and veins, the prana through the breath flows through what is called "Nadis." This is not visible to the naked eye but this can be felt and even seen with the "inner eye of perception" by a person who meditates and whose senses are refined. Science has still not accepted the concept of "Nadis" or energy vessels. "The Nadis penetrate the body from the soles of the feet to the crown of the head. In them is prana, the breath of life and in that life abides consciousness or atma, which is the abode of Energy or Shakti, creatrix of the animate and inanimate worlds" (Varaha Upanishad).

Mental Body (The Emotional Body)

Subtler rather than the gross physical body and the etheric body (pranic body) is the mental body (sometimes referred to as the astral body) which is made up of thoughts. Thoughts are energy and have colour, form, and density just as any physical matter except that it is subtle. The mental body is also comprised of subtle matter which is another form of energy. Hence together with the prana body or the etheric body, this forms the "subtle body." "Manomaya kosha" is the mental sheath, composed of manas, meaning "mind." Instinctual consciousness, thoughts, and perception are all linked to this body and are considered to be a large part in what constitutes the yogic concepts of personality and ego. The mental sheath makes use of the mind, manas, and the five cognitive sense organs – sight, hearing, touch, smell, and taste. It is vaster than the previous two and is all about mental processes – thoughts, ideas, reason, logic, contemplation, feelings, dreams, hopes, and the feelings of good and bad, joy and sorrow, and pleasure and pain.

The Upanishads describe the mind as "the flow of thought" and identify four distinct functions of the mind

1. The emotional mind – wavering emotions and thinking faculty (Manas) – EQ
2. Intellect – the discriminative and learning function (Buddhi) – IQ
3. Memory – the storehouse of information or memory (Chitta) – MQ
4. Ego – the "I" principle (EgQ).

This body is governed by thoughts in the mind, which are considered to have the power to both construct and destroy and most thoughts and actions happen automatically, without conscious control. That is why it is important for us to become in some measure the master of our mind. One way of working with this body (the subconscious mind) is to release or transcend the two outer sheaths through conscious body scans (Yoga Nidra). This allows the programming of the mind to be penetrated and negative patterns to be released and helps in reprogramming the mind. It is at the level of the mental body that the inner senses comprising the emotional mind, the intellect, the ego, and the memory storehouse (Chitta) spring up and begin to perceive, cognize, record, understand, rationalize, discriminate, accept, reject, compare, to name only a few of the myriad functions that it performs effortlessly in our lives. Without this ability to think, feel, etc., we are no better than vegetables.

The mental body is the seat of empirical knowledge. It beholds the world around ("in fact the world is nothing but a projection of the mind" – Ramana Maharishi) and has the capacity to externalize the awareness as well as withdraw it inwards. When it is under the sway of the senses, it is fully occupied with the external impulses that it receives from the world of smells, sounds, lights, colours, touch, and taste. At other times the mind moves inwards when it receives the impulses of the self which help recharge and rejuvenate the mind.

This happens during meditation and helps reach that calm state (often characterized by alpha waves of the mind where productivity and thinking perform at the optimum. For example, alpha waves are at a frequency of 8–13.9 Hz. They are responsible for relaxation, increased learning, memory, concentration, and production of serotonin. Mindfulness meditation and other techniques (such as alpha wave music) which boost brain activity are good because they improve memory, concentration, and learning.

Wisdom Body/Sheath

The wisdom or "Vigyanamaya" sheath along with the previous two sheaths forms the "subtle body" of a human being. This sheath is the layer that connects this and the next or the bliss sheath (causal) body. Without a proper development of the intellect, it is not possible to reach the next state.

Beyond the mental body is the body (sheath) of intuition or Vigyanamaya kosha, and it is subtler than all the preceding bodies. The Taittiriya Upanishad describes the Vigyanamaya kosha in the following manner: "Separate from the self, comprised of mind, there is another inner self comprised of intuitive knowledge. This one is also like the shape of a person like the preceding koshas. Faith is its head, righteousness its right wing and truth its left wing, yoga is its soul, yoga atma, and maha its foundation."

Chitta (Pure Intelligence)

The fourth category of the mind is otherwise called Chitta. Chitta is mind without memory or pure intelligence. This intelligence is like the cosmic intelligence and it simply exists, due to which everything happens. It does not function out of memory, but it simply functions. However, many times it is referred to as stored memory which is not strictly correct. In a way, what one calls the cosmos is a living mind, not in the sense of intellect but in the sense of Chitta. Chitta is the last point of the mind and connects to the basis of creation within oneself as also connects with one's consciousness.

Some of the tools that can be used very effectively to address this body are:

- Deep abdominal breathing and meditation
- Body scans
- Self-affirmation (when one has reached an alpha state through deep breathing and meditation).

The Bliss Body (Sheath)

Vigyananmaya (wisdom) is a very important stage in the ascent of awareness and is the stepping stone to the next stage which is the bliss body or unalloyed happiness, otherwise referred to as the Anandamaya body or a state of perpetual ecstasy (for want of a better term).

I have not dealt with this state in great detail as the focus of our efforts is on the first three bodies which will ensure a stress-free, calm, uncluttered, and sharp mind that is the sine qua non for a knowledge worker.

These five sheaths co-relate to the three bodies that constitute our being. These three bodies are known as gross, subtle, and causal (beyond the causal is the super causal). Along with the sheaths, these bodies influence each and every experience and reaction one faces throughout his/her life.

In modern psychology, the causal body is known as the realm of the unconscious or the psyche of man. It is the mythical Pandora's box, virtually the skeleton in the closet. One cannot know what is stored there until there is awakening in the wisdom sheath. When one experiences awakening in the mental sheath, he/she is still within the realm of the intellect. Everything that one experiences will be within the fold of logic and reason and thus there is a degree of control of the experiences and their outcome. However at the level of wisdom or intuition sheath the intellect is transcended and one enters into the dimension of intuition, where the mind does not work in the ordinary sense. This mind that one is familiar with does not function in Vigyanamaya kosha, wisdom sheath; nor does the intellect as we know it. Each one of us operates at the level of instinct, intelligence, intellect, and intuition. Till the level of intellect, one is under the influence and in the field of the mental sheath. But when the intellect is transcended, even for a second, one will experience flashes of intuition on something the mind has been preoccupied with. History is replete with examples where people have had such flashes of intuition.

The happiness of the body can be strengthened with sleep and meditation. All success is defined as an alignment of our five bodies, namely

1. Body – body quotient (BQ – including the energy quotient)
2. Mind – emotional quotient (EQ)
3. Intellect – intelligence quotient (IQ)
4. Ego – ego quotient (EgQ)
5. Happiness – spiritual quotient (SQ).

KEY TAKEAWAY

In this chapter, we have had an in-depth look at what constitutes our being and what we are made up of and we have attempted to explain the role of the life force. We have explained what the five sheaths are which constitute our being and how each sheath plays a part in making us what we are. We looked at the physical sheath and the life force (Prana) sheath in this chapter. The following chapter therefore looks at the mind (the third sheath) and its constituents in greater detail. The mind is broken up into its constituent parts based on the functions that facilitate better understanding and action. It is normally understood that the mind is located in the brain and without the brain the mind does not function. We look at this aspect, as well as how to control the mind better.

4 Mind Control a Pre-requisite

Bringing awareness to the present moment on a sustained basis is not easy and it requires years of practice, which is why monks spend their lifetime in practicing it. While even a short practice every day has tremendous benefits as witnessed by the results of scientific enquiry, it would be useful to understand what our scriptures have to say on mindfulness and how and why it has benefits in areas such as:

- Stress reduction
- Improving physical and mental health
- Controlling negative emotions
- Leading a happier life
- Reduced reactions to external events
- Providing a means to define a better purpose and meaning in life and leading a more fulfilled life with minimal conflicts
- Moving towards spirituality and in due course an understanding of existential questions such as "who am I," (the proper understanding comprehension of which makes one a more balanced and happier person).

WHAT IS THE MIND?

> Generally in the Western world, the mind is defined as the complex of cognitive faculties that enables consciousness, thinking, reasoning, perception, and judgement – a characteristic of human beings, but which also may apply to other life forms. It is generally agreed that mind is that which enables a being to have subjective awareness and intentionality towards their environment, to perceive and respond to stimuli with some kind of agency, and to have a consciousness, including thinking and feeling. (Wikipedia)

Eastern thoughts, especially the Upanishads, Tantra, and Buddhism, do not accept the above definition and think it is a bit of a mash-up. While the Western psychologists hold the view that the brain enables the mind and that leads to consciousness, Eastern thought says the reverse that it is consciousness that enables the mind (as seen earlier). The second point of divergence is that the above definition makes no differentiation between the mind's functions such as "thinking, reasoning, perception, and judgement." This is very important from a practical perspective, as I will describe later in this chapter, and has implications in practice.

The Upanishads describe the mind as "the flow of thought" and identify four distinct functions of the mind:

- The emotional mind – wavering emotions and thinking faculty (Manas)
- The discriminative and learning function called the intellect (Buddhi)

- The storehouse of information or memory (Chitta)
- The "I" principle or the ego.

This is described in detail later in this chapter.

All attempts at mindfulness, bringing awareness to the present moment and/or focusing the mind, aim at addressing the first function, that of controlling the wavering emotional mind. While in itself it is very beneficial as the tons of research on the subject shows, it is still addressing only part of the "mind" and one could get far greater, deeper, and lasting benefits by a more complete understanding and expansion of the practice. This requires a thorough understanding of all the functions of the mind "holistically" and how they interact with each other as also its evolutes – the five organs of action that perform all activities based on instructions from the mind (through the brain), the five organs of knowledge which get in external stimuli and feed the mind continuously, and the five physiological functions that are controlled by the vital air or the *Prana*. It is postulated in yoga that actions that result from the input mechanism interact at the intellectual level (with the four constituents of the mind) and result in physiological and body reactions and changes. Hence the root of what needs to be treated whether it is to do with issues regarding health, emotions, physiological processes such as digestion and respiration lies in the mind (mental body). Modern neurophysicians are also of the same view and this assertion is currently supported by research. *Prana* (which is the life force energy) is taken in through the breath (the more conscious of the breath we are, more is the *Prana* taken in) and is the bridge between the physical body and the mind which is why breathing exercises have a calming effect on both the body and the mind and therefore emotions. Going further, the discriminative ability between good and bad and right and wrong is a faculty only humans are blessed with and hence this is connected with the intellect. Actions that are filtered through the intellect help to ensure that actions are in line with values and do not result in both internal and external conflicts. Finally, the happiness sheath or body is something that is available to all at the time of sleep since the mind is inactive and hence the pulls and pressures of emotions and memory are absent. It is available in the waking state if one is able to make the mind still even while awake. The more permanent way one can access this is to have the mind totally at one's control through concentration and meditation where the mind is subjugated to one's will and can be used when required.

The constituents of the mind are now described in greater detail as the practices outlined later in this book seek to address each of the 19 constituents individually and collectively for better results.

MANAS – THE EMOTIONAL MIND

"Manas" or the emotional mind is what psychologists usually refer to when talking of the mind. The emotional mind is a huge problem when it is devoid of focus and results in constant chattering that in turn results in further lack of focus and dissipation of energy. In fact, one of the biggest leaks in energy is this constant chattering of the mind. On the other hand, a focused and calm mind conserves and can even add to energy resulting in better decisions and more quality and quantity of output. This is primarily due to the inability or slowness of the mind to learn, the inability to discriminate, and consequently the inability to make wise decisions. It therefore hampers our ability to focus on what we choose because of the various identifications coming into play and our attention being constantly diverted. When the mind is calm, one can go through experiences by examining, analysing, questioning, understanding, and assimilating without going through life mechanically. As one can see, this has a huge bearing and importance for the knowledge worker whose entire productivity, creativity, and effectiveness depend on the output from his mind.

Every leader/knowledge worker needs to understand this. The quality, quantity, and longevity of output depend on how well he/she keeps his/her body and mind in good shape. Traditionally, all mindfulness programs address only this part of the "mind." For greater, deeper, and lasting benefits, what is required is a thorough understanding of all the functions of the mind "holistically" and how they interact with each other as also its evolutes.

The emotional mind can be controlled better through pictures rather than words. That is why, for example, visualizing something works far better than listening to a lecture on the same subject. Pictures appeal to the emotional mind far better.

Some of the exercises for the emotional mind are

- Replacing negative thoughts with positive thoughts
- Self-compassion (kindness and understanding for the hard things in one's life)
- Mindful awareness (resting in the peacefulness of steady and open awareness)
- Bringing to the mind scenes of peace, love, and contentment
- Gratitude – Finding thankfulness and joy even in the hardest times
- Forgiveness – Visualizing forgiving others and oneself
- Feeling balanced, centred, and relaxed
- Abundance – Visualizing creating abundance and prosperity in health, wealth, and success.

BUDDHI – THE INTELLECT

Buddhi is translated as intellect and a sharp intellect is useful in many ways. The use of the intellect is the process of analysis, discernment, logic, and deliberation. Analysis is made of prevailing circumstances with available facts and considering past experiences. Deliberation is the refining of thoughts and imagination, focusing on them and distilling the essence while discernment is the application of logic and cultivating the ability to distinguish between right and wrong and true and false. When these three dimensions of intelligence are harmoniously activated, one will develop the capacity to comprehend and understand any situation and enable one in taking right/good decisions that can withstand the test of time.

The function of the intellect is to discriminate between situations, choices, etc. and effectively decide on what the course of action should be. The emotional mind has an impact on the intellect and vice versa and so does the other parts as well. When one becomes too emotional, he/she finds that his/her discriminative power is impaired, and for one whose intellect is very sharp the emotional mind can be controlled or at least kept in check. Too much garbage stored up in the subconscious or memory also impacts the ability to discriminate because of the overload of conflicting and/or excess information. A sharp intellect with a balanced emotional mind is the key to a knowledge worker's performance. The key question therefore is whether there is a way in which we can sharpen our intellect and the answer is an emphatic "yes." The intellect can be trained to function by keeping our emotional mind in check and under our control and through force of habit consciously training the mind to make informed and thought out decisions.

Developing the intellect requires steadfastness of body and mind and the ability to concentrate and focus the mind. Concentration will increase comprehension and will be dealt with later in great detail because of its importance in developing one's personality. Along with the above, a natural curiosity in asking questions, finding answers, and deliberating on it are other important requisites in developing one's intellect.

CHITTA OR THE SUBCONSCIOUS MIND

Every memory appearing in the mind, whether it is of 5 minutes or 20 years ago, is subsumed under this head. In Eastern spirituality, it is said that even the memory of previous lives is stored here but we will not go into that and restrict our discussion to this life's memories. It is currently an accepted fact that the subconscious forms the largest part of the mind, with the conscious mind contributing to just 2–3% of the total mind. Chitta in a mature person takes the form of pure intelligence without memories. In a normal person, Chitta (loosely put as unconscious memory) has a major role to play because it is from the subconscious or the unconscious that a majority of our thought patterns rise, and unless we clear the cobwebs of the Chitta or the subconscious memory this will continue to hamper our efforts to live in the present. Just look at your own efforts to be in the present and see how easily the mind is distracted with the "noise" and often-times conflicting "thought patterns." It is obviously not easy to enter into the subconscious to clean it of the conflicts that reside there, but through mindful meditation, self-awareness, and conscious breathing it is possible to access the deep recesses of the subconscious mind and some of our fears, anger, and other negative emotion-filled incidents, bring them to the present, and resolve them so that we are not disturbed by the thought patterns that these incidents throw up. Most often we are ourselves not aware of why we react to an incident the way that we do, the answer to which may lie in our past experiences which we have forgotten but which is stored in our subconscious.

AHANKARA OR THE "I" CONSCIOUSNESS OR THE EGO

Ahankara is the identification with "I" as in this body of mine. This identification makes me different from all the other beings in this universe – both human and animals. The intellect directly connects with the third dimension of the mind, called ahankara. Ahankara, or the "ego," gives one a sense of identity. Once the ahankara takes on an identity, the intellect functions only in that context because it is enslaved in that identity. Our identities, such as belonging to a certain nation, community, or whatever else, are necessary for our survival in a particular society. One cannot think beyond this because the intellect from which one is functioning gets its sustenance from ahankara which is the only basis on which the intellect can function. In a normal situation, transcending this is very difficult because that is the nature of the intellect. It needs specified boundaries to function well.

The root cause of all the problems of greed, desire, anger, etc. is this identification that makes me want to ensure that "I" get as much as possible for "myself" or for others with whom I extend this identification. The more one identifies with the universe the more expansive and inclusive are ones' thoughts. One of the key attributes of a successful person who has had an impact on a large number of lives in a positive way and has contributed to society is this concept of an "expanded mind" or the feeling of being connected to the universe. We will not go into the spiritual aspects of this "I" notion which the seers say is false and the root of all problems. However, to the extent that we can expand our consciousness and make it more inclusive it will have positive benefits for society at large as also for the individual in terms of better peace of mind and a more complete and fulfilling life. In fact, research shows that people with strong egos (expanded sense of "I," people with strong self-belief) can be viewed generally as self-confident, secure, emotionally stable, flexible, adaptive, and able to cope well with everyday stresses and frustrations and are more likely to come through as a mature, independent, resourceful, and authentic persons. "On the contrary, those with big egos (narrowly defined as a self-centred person and "full" of themselves) lack inner stability and are more easily upset, tend to be rigid, reactive, dogmatic, and egocentric, simulate self-confidence (rather than truly possess it), display arrogance and a narcissistic sense of entitlement, display deficits in personal integrity and, perhaps more telling than anything else, demonstrate, when feeling threatened, a surprising weakness, even fragility." – Leon F. Seltzer in *Evolution of the Self.*

How does this translate in the workplace. Here is an interesting case study.

Dan Price, an entrepreneur who set up Gravity Payments, revolutionized the industry by offering a minimum wage to his employees of US$70,000 something unheard of in 2011. This caused a media storm, and he became a Harvard case study and a celebrity and created a sensation in industrial circles. But what set him on this path was an interaction he had with one of his entry-level employees named Jason Haley who set him thinking. Haley was a 32-year-old phone tech earning about US$35,000 a year. At a smoking break, Price asked Haley if everything was fine and the response he got was an emphatic NO. While Price was shocked and hurt, to his credit, Price introspected, saw that strict financial discipline bordering on obsession stemmed from circumstances he had faced earlier and decided to change the way he compensated his employees. The rest is history as he created a revolution in the industry with his US$70,000 minimum wage plan. He cut his own salary from US$1.1 million to US$70,000 to help fund it. Price had not only struck a nerve but also turbocharged a debate on how much workers should be paid and whether there should be so much disparity between CEO payments and the rest. This even forced a Walmart to follow suit with increased wages to workers. This is because one person had an expanded view of the self and did not allow his narrow definition of the ego to cloud his decision.

So far, we have been seeing what scriptures have been telling us as also what we have observed from our own experience. In the following few chapters, we will look at how this translates into what science is telling us. In the last few decades, a lot of scientific research has been done to understand the functioning of the brain and its impact on the body and mind as also health and diseases. Science has also been trying to understand how such impact takes place in terms of biochemical processes that happen in certain conditions and situations. This will hopefully give us a better fix in terms of why we should follow certain practices that have withstood the passage of time and how this can help us lead better and more fulfilling lives given the increased uncertainties and stresses of modern-day living.

KEY TAKEAWAY

This chapter examines what constitutes the mind in great detail. We broke up the "mind" as the emotional mind, the intellect, the subconscious (storehouse of information), and the ego (I consciousness) based on the mind's functions. This gives us a better understanding of the mind and how it can be strengthened and controlled by looking at each individual part. Each of the subparts of the mind needs a different approach that has been detailed. Having understood the mind, we move on its physical counterpart (as commonly understood) which is the physical brain. The next chapter examines the functions of the brain and what happens physically when we have different kinds of thoughts and emotions.

5 A Primer on the Brain

WHY AN UNDERSTANDING OF OUR BRAIN IS IMPORTANT?

Modern research shows why some interventions such as meditation, creating a positive joyful mood deliberately and visualization exercises are important. Just dreaming big, having a positive mindset, persisting in one's efforts, and listening to lectures on a topic may not always help one to learn and correct his/her mistakes. Brain imaging has shown that it takes some help from a healthy, sharp brain to achieve one's potential. Let us start with a primer on the physical brain, its functions, and how and what it does.

VIEW OF THE BRAIN

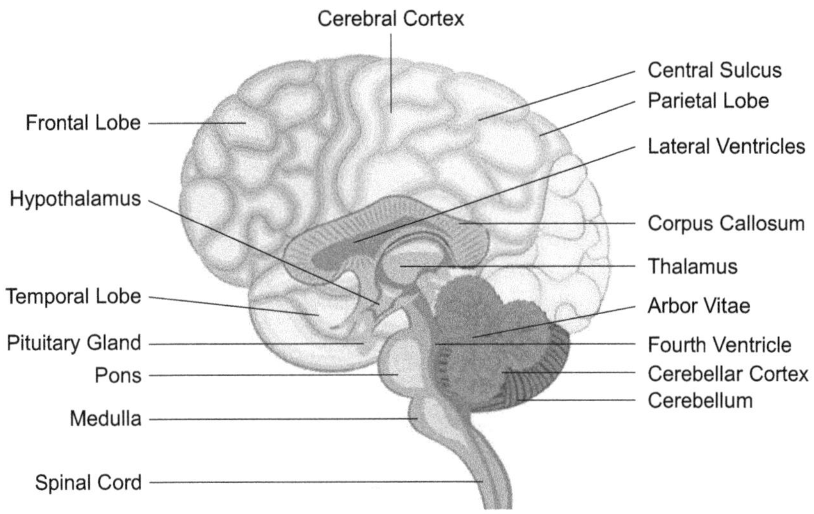

The brain is a complicated piece of equipment. This chapter familiarizes the reader with the description and major parts of the brain to facilitate an understanding of the research findings that have been quoted later.

THREE MAJOR PARTS OF THE BRAIN

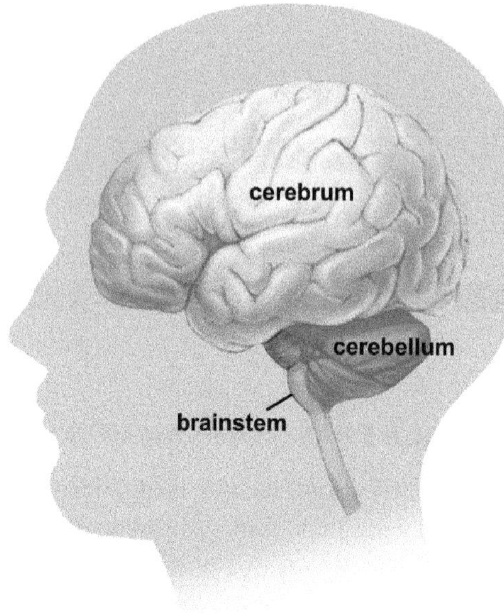

Cerebrum

One of the three major parts of the brain is the cerebrum (the major portion) that consists of the following lobes:

1. Frontal lobe
2. Parietal lobe
3. Occipital lobe
4. Temporal lobe.

These lobes and the description of the functions of each of the lobes are shown in the diagram.

Lobes of the Cerebrum

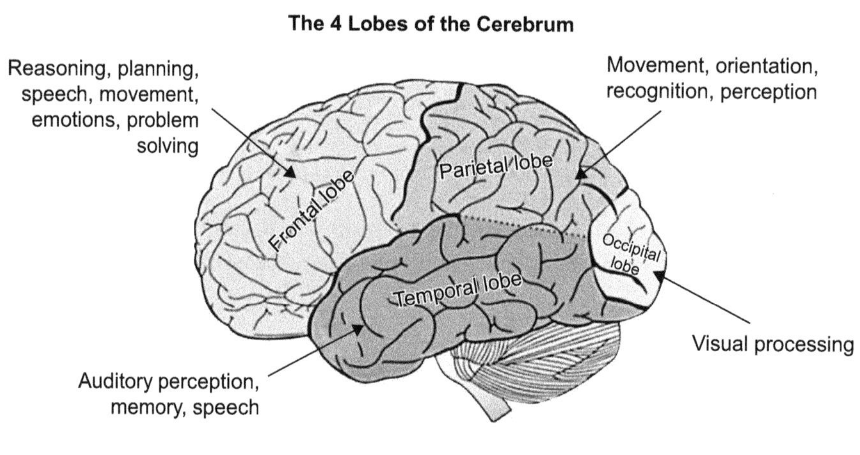

Frontal Lobe

The frontal lobe, from an executive decision-making point of view, is extremely important as it deals with actions such as

- Personality, behaviour, emotions
- Judgement, planning, problem solving
- Speech: speaking and writing
- Body movement (motor strip)
- Intelligence, concentration, self-awareness.

Parietal Lobe

The parietal lobe governs actions such as

- Interpreting language, words
- Sense of touch, pain, temperature (sensory strip)
- Interpreting signals from vision, hearing, motor, sensory, and memory
- Spatial and visual perception.

Occipital Lobe

The occipital lobe primarily interprets vision (colour, light, movement).

Temporal Lobe

The temporal lobe governs areas such as

- Understanding language
- Memory
- Hearing
- Sequencing and organization.

Language

In general, the left hemisphere of the brain is responsible for language and speech and it is called "dominant" hemisphere. The right hemisphere plays a large part in interpreting visual information and spatial processing. In about one-third of people who are left-handed, speech function may be located on the right side of the brain.

Right and Left Brain

The cerebrum is divided into two halves: the right and left hemispheres, both are joined by a bundle of fibres called the corpus callosum that transmits messages from one side to the other. Each hemisphere controls the opposite side of the body. If a stroke occurs on the right side of the brain, one's left arm or leg may be weak or paralysed.

Not all functions of the hemispheres are shared. The left hemisphere controls speech, comprehension, arithmetic, and writing while the right hemisphere controls creativity, spatial ability, artistic, and musical skills. The left hemisphere is dominant in hand use and language in about 92% of people.

Cerebellum

The cerebellum (also called *the little brain*) resembles a smaller version of the cortex because of its densely wrinkled appearance and its halved parts and is responsible for several physical tasks, such as movement, balance, posture, and coordination. Although smaller in size, the cerebellum contains more neurons than the entire brain and is critical for accomplishing day-to-day tasks as simple as walking or sitting down.

Limbic System

The limbic system, also called the "emotional brain," is comprised of four glands that are found inside the cerebrum. The glands help to express emotions and regulate hormonal responses. They are:

- *Amygdala.* The amygdala is responsible for recognition of emotions, memories, and fear. It is located in the telencephalon (the most highly developed section of the cerebrum). It is comprised of two almond-sized pieces of grey matter inside the temporal lobe.
- *Hippocampus.* The hippocampus aids in building memories and cognitive learning. The short-term memories in the hippocampus are converted into permanent ones. The centrally located gland also allows humans to have spatial awareness.
- *Hypothalamus.* This is the master control of the autonomic system. The hypothalamus gland is associated with circadian rhythm (sleep cycles), hunger, and some emotional responses. It is also responsible for regulating pituitary gland and its release of hormones.
- *Thalamus.* A vital piece of grey matter that lives deep within the frontal lobe. The thalamus is responsible for major nervous and sensory functions. With the exception of taste and smell, all senses pass through the thalamus to be categorized into what becomes touch, sight, and hearing.

Brainstem

The brainstem is regarded as the most important part of the entire brain and nervous system and is connected to the spine. It carries out the task of sending messages to all parts of the body. Every physical movement in the body is carried out in some capacity from the brainstem. Even basic functions such as heartbeat and breathing come initially from the brainstem.

There are three parts of the brainstem:

- *Midbrain.* The midbrain is the first section of the brainstem. It is divided into two parts: the *tegmentum* and the *tectum*. It controls functions, such as basic movements, vision, hearing, and eye movement. The midbrain is considered an integral part of the brain that relays messages and contributes to voluntary motor function.
- *Pons.* Any information coming to the brain from the ears passes through the pons first. It is responsible for sensory analysis. Since it is connected to the cerebellum, the pons contributes to movement and posture.
- *Medulla.* Located at the very end of the brainstem, the medulla (also called the *medulla oblongata*) is responsible for controlling functions, such as heartbeat and breathing.

Memory

Memory is a complex process that includes three phases: encoding (deciding what information is important), storing, and recalling. Different areas of the brain are involved in different types of memory. The brain has to pay attention and rehearse in order for an event to move from short-term to long-term memory which is called encoding. This is why repetition ensures long-term recall.

Short-term memory, also called working memory, occurs in the prefrontal cortex. It stores information for about 1 minute and its capacity is limited to about seven items. For example, it enables one to dial a phone number someone mentions. It also intervenes during reading, to memorize the sentence one has read, so that the next one makes sense.

Long-term memory is processed in the hippocampus of the temporal lobe and it is activated when one wants to memorize something for a longer time. This memory has unlimited content and duration capacity. It contains personal memories as well as facts and figures.

Skill memory is processed in the cerebellum, which relays information to the basal ganglia. It stores automatic learned memories such as tying a shoe, playing an instrument, and riding a bike.

SUMMARY

To summarize, the brain consists of the following four parts:

- Cerebrum
- Cerebellum
- Limbic system
- Brainstem.

KEY TAKEAWAY

This chapter has provided a basic understanding of the brain, its parts, and its functions. The following chapter will discuss at some of the scientific research on the brain and its impact on everyday life in as simple manner as possible. It will also examine the neurosciences behind the functioning of the brain and the takeaways from current scientific research.

6 The Neuroscience of Success

KEY TAKEAWAYS FROM CURRENT SCIENTIFIC RESEARCH

The intention of this chapter is to familiarize the reader with some of the more recent advances in the scientific evaluation of meditation and mindfulness practices. While I have quoted some scientific research, I have tried to keep this simple and in a way that a layman can quickly grasp the essence of this body of evidence. The intention is to convince the reader that meditation, mindfulness, and related practices of the East are not unscientific and are currently backed up by solid evidence. The idea is also to try and extend this practice into areas where not much of research has yet been done but going by the current body of evidence it is easy to see the likely benefits that will accrue as a result of its practice.

To facilitate easy reference and aid this discussion, the figure of the brain is shown again.

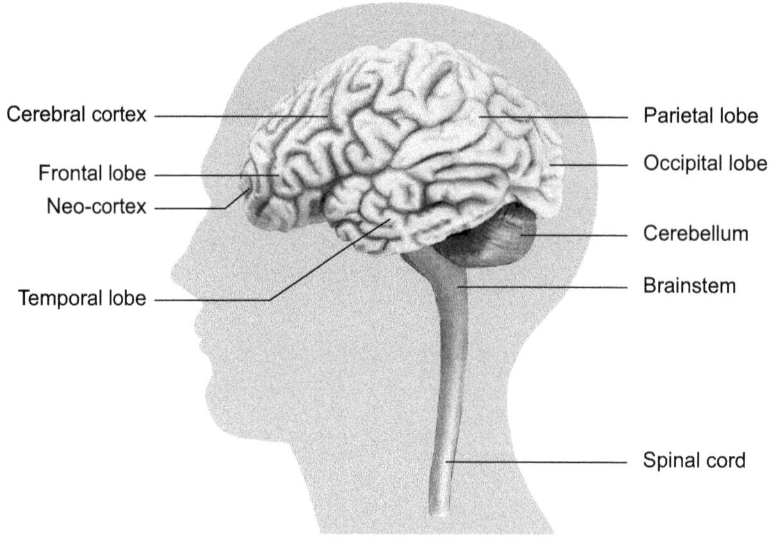

Neuroscience is the systematic, scientific exploration of the human brain. It primarily studies how the 100 or more billion brain cells that trigger electrical impulses operate within the confines of what we call "the brain" and make us conscious beings capable of thought and reasoning. *Applied neuroscience* is a relatively new field that aims to understand the way the brain makes people behave the way they do. It seeks to understand the changes in the brain as people adopt different lifestyles and how they impact thoughts and feelings. It also seeks to understand the impact of such changes in the brain on our actions and outlook. *Neurochemistry* is the science speciality that seeks to understand the chemistry of the nervous system and how it controls behaviour.

ROLE OF NEUROSCIENCES

Scientists, aided by technology, have gained a more accurate view of behaviour and the way it changes because of the integration of psychology (the study of the human mind and human behaviour) and neuroscience (the study of the anatomy and physiology of the brain). Some of these techniques are:

- Functional magnetic resonance imaging (fMRI)
- Positron emission tomography (PET)
- Quantitative electroencephalography (QEEG)
- Single photon emission computed tomography (SPECT).

These studies have revealed neural connections in the living human brain. Advanced computer analysis of these connections has helped researchers develop an increasing body of theoretical work linking the brain (the physical organ) with the human body and the mind (thoughts and feeling which then are translated to action). In other words, science explains the how of the "process," but it still does not have an inkling of the "why."

NEUROTRANSMITTERS

The main chemicals that control behaviour are either neurotransmitters or hormones that either stimulate or calm the person. They also relay signals between nerve cells (neurons). The brain uses neurotransmitters to trigger hormones to convey messages to every part of one's body. They can also affect mood, sleep, concentration, weight, etc. and can cause adverse symptoms when they are out of balance. Neurotransmitter levels are impacted negatively in many ways, most notably by stress, poor diet, neurotoxins, genetic predisposition, drugs, alcohol, nicotine, caffeine, etc.

The main neurotransmitters and their primary impact are as follows:

- *Dopamine* is associated with getting something one wants.
- *Serotonin* is associated with being in a good mood.
- *Oxytocin* is released when trust is growing or when one is falling in love.
- *Noradrenalin* intensifies the effects of all of the above and is involved in attention and concentration.

HORMONES

Hormones are chemicals that carry messages from glands to cells within tissues or organs in the body. They also maintain chemical levels in the bloodstream to help achieve homeostasis, which is a state of stability or balance within the body. The endocrine system manufactures hormones and these chemicals circulate freely in the bloodstream, waiting to be recognized by a target cell responding to an instruction from a neurotransmitter signal. The target cell has a receptor that can be activated only by a specific type of hormone, after which the cell knows to start a certain function within its walls. Genes might get activated, for example, or energy production resumed.

The main hormones and their key associations are:

- *Cortisol* – Related to stress levels.
- *Adrenalin* – Crucial part of the body's fight-or-flight response.

- *Testosterone* – Associated with negative behavioural effects, such as aggression or dominance (associated more with male behaviour).
- *Oestrogen/progesterone* – Associated with female reproduction.

Both the neurotransmitters and the hormones work together. Neurotransmitters are an electrical current generated in a nerve cell to make them effective. Hormones are released by the demands of neurochemical signals directly into the bloodstream from ductless glands around the body (the endocrine system) and are necessary in the right quantities and in the right places to make things work effectively. One way of thinking about the neurotransmitters is that they act directly on the emotions and trigger the hormones, while the hormones act directly on the body. In practice, both are seamless and integrated.

Our endocrine system is shown in the figure.

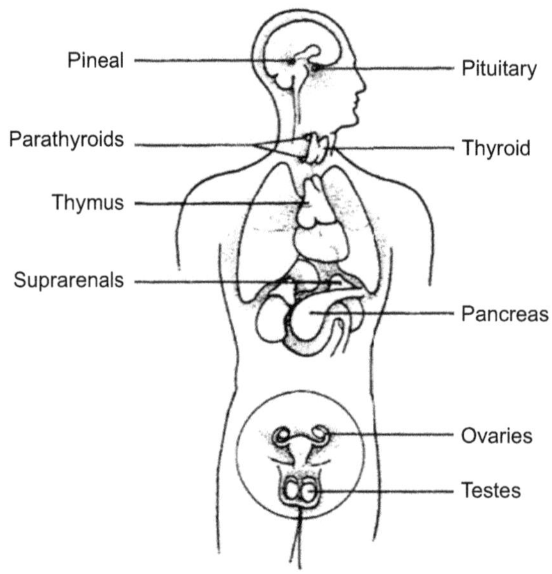

Endocrine glands

The endocrine system helps to maintain the body's homeostasis (balance). Metabolism, growth, sexual development, mental growth, mineral balance, heart rate regulation, setting our sleep cycle, and muscular and skeletal growth are some of the functions of the endocrine gland. The hypothalamus is a part of brain that is responsible for the direct control of endocrine system through the pituitary gland. It is also the centre of emotions and is affected by strong emotions, odour, powerful thoughts, taste, stress, laughter, etc.

According to science, the pituitary gland is the master gland controlling the entire endocrine system that includes the pineal gland, thyroid gland, parathyroid gland, thymus gland, adrenal glands, pancreas, ovaries, and testes which are all parts of the endocrine system. The hypothalamus sends a signal to the pituitary gland which then releases chemicals to stimulate the hormones from other endocrine glands. Science has still not understood the full functioning of the pineal gland which as per Eastern spirituality is the master organ of the human body that connects the material body with the spiritual self and is like a step down transformer that helps connect the universe with the individual self. However, there are currently more scientific evidence of the importance of the pineal gland.

Sara Lazar, a neuroscientist at Harvard Medical School, used MRI technology to look at very fine detailed brain structures and see what is happening to the brain while a person is performing a certain task, including yoga and meditation. In her research, Lazar looked at individuals with extensive meditation experience that involved focused attention on internal experiences (no mantras or chanting). The research also indicated that long-term meditation practice is associated with altered resting electroencephalogram patterns, which is indicative of long-lasting changes in brain activity. The research hypothesized that meditation practice might also be associated with changes in the brain's physical structure. MRI was used to assess cortical thickness in 20 participants with extensive insight meditation experience, which involved focused attention to internal experiences. This showed that brain regions associated with attention, perception, and sensory processing were thicker in meditation participants than the control group, including the pre-frontal cortex (PFC) and right anterior insula (RAI). Differences in PFC thickness were most pronounced in older participants, suggesting that meditation might offset age-related cortical thinning. Finally, the thickness of two regions correlated with meditation experience. These data provide the first structural evidence for experience-dependent cortical plasticity associated with meditation practice.

In her next study, Lazar engaged people who had never meditated before and put them through a Mindfulness-Based Stress Reduction training programme, where they took a weekly class and were told to perform mindfulness exercises, including body scan, mindful yoga, and sitting meditation for 30–40 minutes every day. Lazar wanted to test the participants for positive effects of mindfulness meditation on their psychological well-being and alleviating symptoms of various disorders such as anxiety, depression, eating disorder, insomnia, or chronic pain.

After 8 weeks, Lazar found out that the brain volume increased in four regions, of which the most relevant were:

- Hippocampus is a seahorse-shaped structure responsible for learning, storage of memories, spatial orientation, and regulation of emotions.
- The temporoparietal junction (TPJ) is the area where temporal and parietal lobes meet, and it is responsible for empathy and compassion.

On the other hand, the area where brain volume decreased was the amygdala which is responsible for triggering the fight-or-flight response as a reaction to a threat, whether real or only perceived. The decrease in grey matter correlated with changes in the levels of stress. The smaller their amygdala became, the less stressed people felt, even though their external environment remained the same. It proved that the change in amygdala reflected the change in the people's reactions to their environment, not in the environment itself.

To understand the relationship between cognition and emotion, a study was done by Beauregard *et al.* (2001) which was published in *Journal of Neuroscience*, in which brain activation was measured in normal male subjects while they either responded in a normal manner to erotic film excerpts or voluntarily attempted to inhibit the sexual arousal induced by viewing erotic stimuli. Results demonstrated that the sexual arousal experienced, in response to the erotic film excerpts, was associated with activation in "limbic" and paralimbic structures, such as the right amygdala, right anterior temporal pole, and hypothalamus. In addition, the attempted inhibition of the sexual arousal generated by viewing the erotic stimuli was associated with activation of the right superior frontal gyrus and right anterior cingulate gyrus. No activation was found in limbic areas. These findings reinforce the view that emotional self-regulation is normally implemented by a neural circuit comprising various prefrontal regions and subcortical limbic structures. They also suggested that humans have the capacity to influence the electrochemical dynamics of their brain by voluntarily changing the nature of the mind processes unfolding in the psychological space.

SOME LEARNINGS FROM NEUROSCIENCE

Some of the key learnings from neuroscience are summarized as follows:

- The brain is wired to minimize danger and maximize reward.
- The human brain is an intensely social organ.
- No two brains are the same and the brain is programmed based on thoughts and action.
- It is intensely malleable (called neuroplasticity) throughout its lifetime, against all conventional wisdom.
- Attention (awareness) can change the brain.
- Emotions can be passed on.
- Our attention spans are very limited.

SOME MYTHS BUSTED (BASED ON SCIENTIFIC RESEARCH)

Neuroscience has also helped bust some long-held positions that include the following:

- The injured brain cannot heal itself.
- Aging of the brain is inevitable, time related, and irreversible.
- The brain loses millions of cells a day and these cells cannot be replaced.
- The reactions of the limbic system (lower/reptilian brain) – fear, anger, and aggression – cannot be overruled by the higher brain.
- The left brain is the more dominant brain.

FACTS ABOUT THE BRAIN

Some key facts of the brain which are important to note and can help us plan our lives better are:

- The brain thrives with exercise and rest (not necessarily sleep).
- Emotions stimulate the brain the most.
- The brain is affected by stress.
- Sight is the sense that stimulates the brain the most.
- The brain develops more if there is curiosity.

WHAT IS THE MAIN DRIVER OF CHANGE IN OUR BRAIN?

Neuroplasticity is the ability of the brain to develop and adapt throughout one's life. This means that the brain has the innate ability to either improve its functioning or degrade depending on how much it is used and which parts of the brain are excited.

In the past, the belief was that after adolescence, the brain stopped growing and there was a gradual decline later. Research has conclusively proved that the old belief is not true and the brain is a continuously changing organ and can be trained to learn new things throughout the lifetime.

Neuroscientist Lara Boyd from the University of British Columbia pointed out that the human brain changes in three ways to support learning of new things:

1. *Chemical* – Transfer of chemical signals between neurons, which is linked to short-term improvement (e.g. of a memory or a motor skill).
2. *Structural* – Changes in connections between neurons, which are linked to long-term improvement. It means that the brain regions that are important for specific behaviours may change their structure or

enlarge. These changes need more time to take place, which underlines the importance of a dedicated practice (Indian yogic thought puts it as about 41 days of continuous practice to create new neural pathways based on meditation, observation, and experience).

3. *Functional* – Increased excitability of a brain region in relation to a certain behaviour.

In essence, the more one uses a particular brain region, the easier it is to trigger its use again.

> Repeat those behaviours that are healthy for your brain and break those behaviours and habits that are not. Practice… and build the brain you want. – Lara Boyd, PT, PhD

QUANTUM SCIENCE AND NEUROBIOLOGY

In the normal world, an object such as a ball can only be in one place at one time. But in the quantum world, a particle such as an electron can occupy an infinite number of places *at the same time*, existing in what physicists call a superposition of multiple states. In the quantum world two individual particles such as photons *can* be entangled, such that the mere act of sensing one photon with a detector instantaneously forces the other photon, no matter how far away, to assume a particular state. Such entanglement means that in the quantum universe, multiple distinct entities can sometimes behave as a single entity, no matter how far apart the distinct entities are. These "impossible" behaviours make quantum entities ideal for doing the impossible with, for example, computers. In normal computers a stored bit of information is either 0 or 1, but in a quantum computer a stored bit, called a qubit (quantum bit), is both 0 and 1 at the same time. Thus, where a simple memory store of 8 bits can contain any individual number from 0 to 255 ($2^8 = 256$) a memory of 8 qubits can store $2^8 = 256$ *separate numbers* all at once! The ability to store exponentially more information is why quantum computers promise a quantum leap in processing power.

The intersection of quantum science and neurobiology is an extremely engaging field because the human brain is a far more powerful and complicated processor. If the brain can operate in a quantum way, then its power increases manifold. Physicists are currently coming around to the view that it is within the realms of possibility since the underlying consciousness is the basis of the human brain (as per yogic thought) and this increases the power of the brain in a quantum leap.

In May 2018, a research team at Groningen University that included physicist Thomas la Cour Jansen found evidence that plants and some photosynthetic bacteria achieve nearly 100% efficiency converting sunlight to usable energy by exploiting the fact that absorption of solar energy causes some electrons in light-capturing molecules to simultaneously exist in both excited and non-excited quantum states spread across relatively long distances inside the plant, allowing the light-excited electrons to find the most efficient path from the molecules where light is captured to different molecules where usable energy for the plant is created. The discovery of quantum effects in plant biology has given rise to an entirely new field of science called quantum biology. In the past few years, quantum biologists have unearthed evidence of quantum mechanical properties in magnetic field perception in the eyes of some birds (enabling the birds to navigate during migration), and in the activation of smell receptors in humans. Vision researchers have also discovered that photoreceptors in the human retina are capable of generating electrical signals from the capture of a single quantum of light. Neuroscientists are currently investigating the possibility of brains generating usable energy or transmitting and storing information among neurons using quantum effects such as superposition and entanglement. This is the nascent field of quantum neuroscience, an exciting new area that could give rise to a better understanding of the human brain and possibly some insights to the question of "why" the brain behaves the way it does.

An interesting question that needs to be researched is whether meditation opens up possibilities for the brain (awareness) to achieve quantum effects where one can connect with people far away without the need for any network? Whether it is possible to impact someone else's thinking by connecting to them through the power of the mind?

IS HAPPINESS A GIFT OR A DEVELOPED SKILL?

Based on current research, it is quite obvious that happiness is a skill (or a state) that can be cultivated and the brain can be trained through practices such as meditation and mindfulness. How much of meditation in terms of time is a matter that still needs to be researched in detail?

Scientists from the Centre for Healthy Minds at the University of Wisconsin-Madison define well-being from the viewpoint of the following four areas:

1. *Sustained positive emotion.* In a study that examined response to positive images, individuals with higher activity in those brain regions linked to positive emotions reported a higher level of psychological well-being.
2. *Recovery from negative emotion.* There is evidence that mindfulness training leads to greater resilience to painful stimuli. In this study, experienced meditators reported the same pain intensity but with less unpleasantness as compared to as individuals with little mindfulness experience, but less unpleasantness.
3. *Pro-social behaviour and generosity.* Behaviour that increases social bonds and improves the quality of social relationships increases well-being. Research then suggests that compassion can be cultivated with mental training.
4. *Mindfulness and mind wandering.* Mindfulness, defined as paying attention to the present moment without judgement, makes people happier. A study (Harvard psychologists Matthew A. Killingsworth and Daniel T. Gilbert) where a smartphone app was used to monitor people's thoughts, feelings, and actions showed that their minds were wandering approximately half of the time, and while doing so they reported significantly more unhappiness.

The human brain is extremely plastic and establishes new neural connections daily. These intricate networks, however, need to be reinforced and consolidated through our behaviour, similar to a path through a forest that needs to be walked; otherwise, it will be grown over and eventually disappear.

IMPORTANT LESSONS BASED ON SPECT

Four important lessons about the brain that show why it is instrumental to a person's success (based on more than 135,000 SPECT, imaging of brains from people of more than 90 countries by Amen Clinics).

- Protect the most human, thoughtful part of one's brain.
- Safeguard one's brain's pleasure centres.
- Know how to keep one's brain and memory healthy for a lifetime.
- One is not stuck with the brain he/she has. He/she can make it better.

Protect the Most Human, Thoughtful Part of One's Brain

The PFC involved in complex behaviours and personality development accounts for 30% of the brain's volume (in comparison, 11% in chimpanzees, 7% in dogs, 3% in cats, and 1% in mice). The PFC is involved in executive functions, such as focus, forethought, judgement, impulse control, and empathy, and functions like the boss at work. When the PFC is low in activity, people struggle to make good decisions. In situation where the PFC activity is low, the PFC protects the brain, particularly from brain injuries.

Safeguard the Brain's Pleasure Centres

The nucleus accumbens that is situated deep within the recesses of both hemispheres of the brain is involved with pleasure and motivation. This is intensely activated by dopamine and substances such as cocaine, sex, video games, high fat and sugary foods, and fame. Dopamine fuels addiction, making everyday activities less interesting. Intense pleasure means huge dopamine dumps, which over time causes the nucleus accumbens to be less responsive, consequently causing the need for more and more of the behaviours. One can protect these pleasure centres by limiting thrill-seeking activities, such as racing, cocaine, methamphetamines, excessive video games, pornography, and scary movies, which could wear them out. Safer behaviours, such as sunlight, exercise, meditation, and listening to pleasurable music, protect the brain and also help cushion these pleasure centres. *Having a dedicated passion and purpose in life* also helps to activate the pleasure centres in a healthy way.

Keep the Brain and Memory Healthy for a Lifetime

Illnesses, such as Alzheimer's disease and other forms of dementia, begin in the brain year, even decades, before people have any symptoms. Hence work to keep brain healthy with proper diet and physical and mental exercises. Meditation is especially useful in keeping Alzheimer's at bay.

Brain can be Made Better

The study by Amen Clinics on active and retired NFL players saw high levels of brain damage in players. Most of them had been hit in the head thousands of times. Eighty per cent of the players showed improvement in less than 2 months on their Memory Rescue programme. This shows that the brain can be changed and improved at any stage and protecting the brain is crucial for one's health and success.

KEEPING THE BRAIN HEALTHY

Daniel Goleman's wonderful book, *Memory Rescue*, indicates some important ways to keep the brain healthy. These include

- *Blood flow*: Low blood flow is the primary brain imaging predictor of Alzheimer's disease. Strategies to increase blood flow include regular exercise and consuming beets.
- *Retirement/aging*: New learning should be part of everyone's life. When learning stops, the brain starts dying.
- *Genetics*: Genes are not a death sentence, but they should be a wake-up call. Those who are prone by genetics should be extra careful and take appropriate steps.
- *Head trauma*: The brain is soft while the skull is hard with sharp bony ridges. It is prudent to protecting it from falls, getting hit with helmets, and avoiding dangerous activities that put the head in danger.
- *Toxins, drugs, alcohol, environmental toxins such as mould*: Support the four organs of detoxification with simple steps: drinking more water to flush out the kidneys, eating more fibre to help the gut along, sweating more to wring out the toxins with exercise or saunas, and detoxifying the liver with hefty amounts of vegetables.
- *Mental health issues*: Managing depression and chronic stress with professional help and meditation.
- *Immunity and infections*: Optimizing the vitamin D level to help protect against inflammatory diseases such as Lyme disease.
- *Neurohormone deficiencies*: Regularly test and optimize hormones if one has a history of thyroid problems or testosterone imbalances.
- *Diabesity*: This term is used to explain the condition that comes from a combination of high blood sugar and overweight. It can be controlled by eating a calorie-smart diet, filled with colourful fruits and vegetables, protein, and fat. Brain function relies on good fat to perform at optimal levels.
- *Sleep issues*: Sleep apnoea or chronic insomnia can interrupt brain function and make it hard to be productive. This needs to be managed.

THE RETICULAR ACTIVATING SYSTEM

The reticular activating system (RAS) is one of the most important parts of the brain and is located at the base of the brain where it connects with the spinal cord. RAS influences cognition and acts as a filter before a message enters the cerebrum where it is then converted into conscious thoughts, emotions, or even both. Even though the cerebrum is the centre of thought, it will not respond to a message unless the RAS allows it. In that sense, the RAS is similar to Google that helps to filter the millions of websites and to filter out those that one is not interested in simply by typing a keyword (Ruben Gonzalez, author of *The Courage to Succeed*).

Messages that are currently important get through. For example, if one is focused on preparing for a speaking engagement then the RAS is going to filter in the thoughts that are going to make the presentation a success, such as the tools and resources needed to deliver a memorable speech. What this practically means is that the more one keep one's goals "top of mind," the more the subconscious mind will work to reach them. That is why writing one's goals down every day, visualizing the intended outcome, and *regularly saying affirmations* are so important! Doing those things truly helps one to focus on his/her subconscious mind on what is important to him/her. All these practices have been part of the Eastern meditation from time immemorial, currently supported by scientific research.

DOPAMINE FEEDBACK LOOPS

While RAS helps one focus on the desired outcome, the release of dopamine makes success feel good. When one succeeds at something, the brain releases chemical rewards, the most important of which is the neurotransmitter dopamine. Dopamine produces the sensation of pleasure whenever one tastes coffee or chocolate, or when one achieves a big win. That is why one feels high after a win, and it is not just psychological but biochemical.

Dopamine is addictive and is strongly connected to motivation. It drives us to repeat the behaviours that create that rush, even when we are not experiencing it. However, the catch is that dopamine loops make repeated success less pleasurable, resulting in the seeking for bigger rewards and the drive to seek out ever-greater thrills. This is the reason why video game players are constantly engaged and one checks the phone every minute after updating one's Facebook status. Dopamine motivates people in accomplishing bigger and better things. For example, if a salesman's goal was to acquire three new clients within 2 weeks, then the next goal would be to acquire say five or six new clients in 1 week. Everything else is the same, except the more challenging, and rewarding, task of doubling one's stable of clients. As an added perk, this also helps one weed out the work and goals that are not motivating enough.

REWRITING MEMORIES

According to neuroscientists, the way that the brain retrieves memories can also determine success. For example, if once one starts and fails at a business, one is more hesitant about taking that risk again.

Scientists, however, found that those bad memories can be edited to remove the negative associations. In fact, this memory therapy is used to treat post-traumatic stress disorder (PTSD) sufferers. One can also edit good memories to further propel success.

What needs to be done to weaken bad memories is to bring that memory back and then let it get smaller and dimmer. This is exactly what mindful meditation is all about – live in the moment, bring in that memory to this moment, and then observe and make edits as required. The old memories will no longer come back to haunt as the brain cannot distinguish between an actual incident that happened in the past and is stored in the subconscious and the new memory that is currently the basis of action. It is like one watching a small black-and-white TV fade out (as an independent observer). Once there, insert new details that scramble the memory. For instance, think about a bombed investor pitch. Now change the setting, insert new incidents, and make it more humorous. A few times of such visualization will change the memory and reduce the feeling of failure that is stored. Similarly for strengthening memories, recall the good memories as bright and loud as possible and keep strengthening the experience.

This is validation of mindful meditation supplemented with use of visualization to change stored memories and erase the subconscious. This will also help to erase troubling memories that have an impact on responses to current situations and to manage phobias and the like.

REWIRING ONE'S BRAIN FOR SUCCESS

The brain can be rewired to make it attuned to success. In fact, according to neuroscientist Michael Merzenich, it takes just 30 hours of training based on specific neuroscience techniques to improve memory and cognition, speech patterns, and reading comprehension. That is just an hour a day for a month to achieve lifelong success. The training involves simple daily tasks such as:

- *Exercise and meditation.* Exercise releases endorphins, which can help with problem solving and boost creativity. Meditation can help one to achieve inner calm and break down any mental barriers or limitations.
- *Consuming a diet rich in omega-3 fats and healthy fats.* This can help keep dopamine levels in the brain active, as well as increase cerebral circulation.
- *Precision affirmations.*

  "Repeat positive statements to ourselves in order to believe it," said John Assaraf, the CEO of NeuroGym. "While that may sound good in theory, there is often a severe lack of specificity that can hinder results." Instead, "make a clear, definitive statement about yourself as if it is already true, your subconscious mind takes over and will act in accordance with that belief." This "will imprint these beliefs into new neural pathways."

- *Saying "Chief Aim" every morning and evening.* Based on Napoleon Hill's *Think and Grow Rich*, "A definite chief aim is a specific, clearly-defined statement of purpose," wrote Dr. Julie Connor. "It has the power to guide your subconscious mind. It transforms your attitude from pessimism into positive expectation." One has to write down his/her own "chief aim" and say it out loud every morning and evening.
- *Getting plenty of rest.* What is required is rest for the brain (not necessarily sleep) and meditation is the best way.
- Carve out 15 minutes of each day to learn something new or master a skill that one already has. It will have a positive impact on his/her brain.
- *Distancing from negative and stressful environments.* According to Robert Sapolsky, a neuroendocrinology professor at Stanford University, "stress can not only be stopped, but reversed once the source, psychological or physical, is removed or sufficiently reduced." In other words, the physical environment around us plays a very important role in the health of our brain.
- *Visualization.* Visualization is a powerful tool to retrain the subconscious mind, because it allows one to feel and experience a situation which has not happened yet – as if it were real. Dreams/visualization precedes reality.

NEUROPLASTICITY AND BRAIN AGILITY

- According to neuroscientists, everything one has experienced in his/her life has moulded and shaped his/her brain to favour certain behaviours and habits. But those behaviours and habits may not be optimal.
- By focusing attention on and repeatedly practicing new, desirable behaviours, leaders can redirect their brains' chemical, hormonal, and physical resources to create new pathways. The old ones, meanwhile, wither from lack of use.
- Learning, particularly attention, heavy subjects like a language or a musical instrument is the best way to enhance plasticity. "The fact that you are forced to attend to things that your brain hasn't experienced before has its own benefit apart from what you learn. The brain becomes more flexible, which [supports] things like being able to regulate your emotions, solve complex problems, and think more creatively."
- To be nimble, one must think nimbly. Brain agility is the ability to switch seamlessly among different ways of thinking: from the logical to the intuitive and to the creative. Agility may be particularly important for entrepreneurs. "The fact that the brain is likely to think in diverse ways or absorb diverse ideas means that you are more likely to spot trends, pivot, be ahead of the curve."
- Multitaskers who try to use several modes of thinking at once generally do less well at all of them. Neuroscientists recommend working on problems consecutively and looking at them from different angles. Leaders can also leverage different thinking styles within their teams.

KEY TAKEAWAY

To summarize, research has currently established that meditation and mindfulness practices have the following impact. It increases the grey matter in the:

- Insula – interoception; self-awareness; empathy for emotions.
- Hippocampus – visual–spatial memory; establishing context; inhibiting amygdala and cortisol.
- PFC – executive functions; attention control.
- Reduced cortical thinning with aging in insula and PFC.
- Increased activation of left frontal regions lifts mood. Increased gamma-range brainwaves may be associated with integration and peace.
- The key findings in layman term supports what yogic thought has been saying that the attitudes, such as peace, calmness, focus, benevolence, gratitude, and forgiveness, can all be learnt through meditation and awareness at any stage of one's life. It takes about 41 days for a neural pathway to be created which is why most ancient practices emphasize this number for fasting or for changing habits. Having once formed a neural pathway, practice is the key to sustain that pathway.

This chapter discussed at the neurosciences behind the functioning of the brain and the takeaways from the current scientific research. The next chapter expands on this theme and looks at how neuroplasticity of the brain is perhaps something that we can leverage for immense benefit which is enumerated and can be done through meditation. These chapters help in understanding issues such as the benefits of meditation from a scientific perspective, erasing one's mental stereotypes, and redefining one's identity based on meditation practices.

7 Harness Neuroplasticity through Meditation

According to a highly referenced article (Julianne *et al.*, 2010) with more than 300,000 views, published in the esteemed *PLOS Medicine* journal, people with the most social relationships (both quantity and quality) are not only much happier, but also live longer (>50%). Another study by UCLA Professor of Medicine Dr. Steve Cole showed that "feeling connected" to others strengthens immunity.

Neuroscientists said that when we feel isolated and separated from the "whole," one particular brain region (the "parietal lobe") becomes overheated. A scientist from University of Pennsylvania, Dr. Andrew Newberg, took brain images of Tibetan monks during meditation. As expected, their "highly intelligent" frontal lobes lit up the screen, similar to other studies. However, what surprised him most was that the meditators' "three-dimensional"-based parietal lobes cooled off immensely, which is the same area that loneliness and social isolation brings to a boil.

Steve Jobs reflected in Walter Isaacson's much-discussed biography of him, one of the best biographies and memoirs of 2011:

> The people in the Indian countryside don't use their intellect like we do, they use their intuition instead, and the intuition is far more developed than in the rest of the world ... Intuition is a very powerful thing, more powerful than intellect, in my opinion. That's had a big impact on my work. Western rational thought is not an innate human characteristic, it is learned and it is the great achievement of Western civilization. In the villages of India, they never learned it. They learned something else, which is in some ways just as valuable but in other ways is not. That's the power of intuition and experiential wisdom. You get your intuition back when you make space for it, when you stop the chattering of the rational mind. The rational mind doesn't nourish you. You assume that it gives you the truth, because the rational mind is the golden calf that this culture worships, but this is not true. Rationality squeezes out much that is rich and juicy and fascinating.

A similar sentiment is attributed to Albert Einstein, "The intuitive mind is a sacred gift and the rational mind is a faithful servant. We have created a society that honours the servant and has forgotten the gift."

Quoted below are some of the positive effects of meditation based on several studies.

CORPUS CALLOSUM – CREATIVITY AND BRAIN POWER INCREASES THROUGH MEDITATION

The corpus callosum is the primary commissural region of the brain consisting of white matter tracts that connect the left and right cerebral hemispheres. The main function of the corpus callosum is the communication between the two hemispheres and the different parts of the corpus callosum connect similar areas of each hemisphere.

Brain imaging studies have shown that highly successful, massively creative people use both brain halves in a much more balanced and integrated way than the rest of us. A 2012 UCLA School of Medicine study (bridging the hemispheres in meditation: thicker callosal regions and enhanced fractional anisotropy (FA) in long-term practitioners [Luders *et al.*, 2012]) found that the "corpus callosum" was remarkably stronger, thicker, and more well connected in meditation practitioners.

In an experimental study at Erasmus University in Rotterdam, the Netherlands, 129 students were divided into three groups, assigned a creative task, and asked to generate as many business ideas as possible.

Before the individual brainstorming began, the first group participated in a 10-minute audio-guided mindfulness meditation and the second group participated in a 10-minute fake meditation exercise (i.e. they were instructed to think freely by letting their minds wander). The third group started to brainstorm immediately.

Each of the three groups generated roughly the same number of ideas, and the length of the descriptions of the ideas was similar. The main difference was that meditators came up with a much wider range of ideas. The meditators demonstrated a 22% wider range of ideas than the two non-meditating groups.

It was also found that a short meditation, similar to physical exercise, often put people in a more positive and relaxed frame of mind. In the group that had meditated, most people felt less negative. In particular, meditation decreased participants' feeling of restlessness (by 23%), nervousness (by 17%), and irritation (by 24%).

HIPPOCAMPUS – DEPRESSION CAN BE KEPT IN CHECK WITH MEDITATION AND MEMORY AND LEARNING CAN BE ENHANCED

Hippocampus is the region of the brain that is associated primarily with memory and it is responsible for processing of long-term memory and emotional responses. Globally, in 2019, more than 264 million people of all ages suffer from depression and this is a leading cause of disability worldwide. It is reported that more women are affected by depression than men. The number of randomized controlled trials, the gold standard for clinical study, involving mindfulness has jumped from 1 in the period 1995–1997 to 11 in 2004–2006, to a whopping 216 in 2013–2015, according to a recent article summarizing scientific findings on the subject. In cases of depression, chronic pain, and anxiety, well-designed and well-run studies have shown benefits for patients engaging in a mindfulness meditation programme, with effects similar to other existing treatments, a landmark in Washington University School of Medicine study (Sheline *et al.*, 1999). MRI imaged the brains of 48 women, half of which were suffering from major clinical depression. They found that as against the control group, the "hippocampi" of the depressed patients had atrophied significantly, with a clear link between "number of years depressed" and degree of shrinkage. A 2008 study published in the *Neuroimage* journal found that after only 8 weeks of meditation, the left and right "hippocampi" of participants had significantly grown in neural thickness, density, and overall size.

This interesting finding means that one can reverse depression through adding meditation to one's daily routine. Dr. Larry Squire, a world-renowned psychiatrist from University of California, San Diego, published a groundbreaking study titled "Memory, Hippocampus, and Brain Systems," illustrating how critical the "hippocampus" is to learning and memory.

As one of the most prominent neuroscientists in the world, Dr. Sara Lazar with her colleagues from Harvard University has studied the meditating brain for decades. Her research (mindfulness practice leads to increases in regional brain grey matter density) shows that meditation dramatically increases "hippocampal cortical thickness," with magnitude determined by experience.

Dr. Emma Seppala, a Science Director at Stanford and a Co-Director and Lecturer at Yale, has researched the psychology of happiness combined with the findings of academic research with the personal accounts of various business owners and executives to argue that meditation has real benefits for CEOs and everyone else. This study was published in *Harvard Business Review* in its issue dated December 2015. The article focuses on benefits that such an audience would be expected to prioritize, such as productivity, creativity, and reduced stress.

PFC – MEDITATION MAKES ONE SMART AND HEALTHY

The PFC is the section of the frontal cortex that lies at the very front of the brain. The PFC makes up over 10% of the volume of the brain, and thus it is involved in many functions of cognition most notably in the executive function. In general, executive functions focus on controlling short-sighted, reflexive behaviours to take part in activities such as planning, decision-making, problem-solving, self-control, and acting with long-term goals in mind.

A landmark 2005 study by a Harvard neuroscientist Dr. Sara Lazar found that experienced meditators had much more neural density, thickness, folds, and electrical activity within their PFC.

AMYGDALA – HOW MEDITATION TRANSFORMS ONE'S STRESS RESPONSE AND ENDS ANXIETY

As we have seen earlier, the amygdala is an almond-shaped structure in the brain located closely to the hippocampus in the frontal portion of the temporal lobe. The amygdala is essential to feel certain emotions and to perceive them in other people. It is responsible for the perception of emotions such as anger, fear, and sadness, as well as control of aggression and it helps to store memories of events and emotions so that an individual may be able to recognize similar events in the future. Flight or fight response and aggressive reactions are primarily triggered by the amygdala. A number of studies point to stress that is the major cause of disease and disability. It is therefore important to find out a way to reduce the role the amygdala plays in our daily lives. In 2011, the researchers from Massachusetts General Hospital brain-scanned 51 adults using fMRI before and after 8 weeks of mindful meditation training and found that the new meditators had effectively silenced the "electrical activity" within their primitive amygdala(e), and in effect had far fewer "anxiety, worry, and fear signals" bouncing around. However, what shook the neuroscientific community to the core was that the participants had dramatically decreased the size/volume of their amygdala(e) in less than 2 months of meditation.

The implications of this finding are tremendous. We can reduce stress levels in this Covid-19 situation by doing a little bit of meditation. The negative effects of stress such as anxiety, depression, and addiction can all be controlled without medication.

ANTERIOR INSULA – MEDITATION MAKES ONE KIND AND HAPPY

The insula is a small region of the cerebral cortex located deep within the lateral sulcus, which is a large fissure that separates the frontal and parietal lobes from the temporal lobe. The insula is involved in pain, love, emotion, craving, addiction, enjoyment of music, and even the tasting of wine.

A.D. Craig, an American neuroanatomist and neuroscientist, who developed a hypothesis that the insula is the cornerstone of our overall awareness, suggested that the insula constantly receives a heaping of information about the location and condition of our bodies, our subjective emotions, and the key features of our environment. It then incorporates the salient, or important, information into what Craig called a "global emotional moment." A global emotional moment is an image of ourselves at one point in time which includes all of the information that is important to us (e.g. I am happy, stimulated, yet hungry). According to Craig, it is the stringing together of these global emotional moments that allow us to be subjectively aware of the present moment, and it all happens in the insula.

> The anterior insular cortex (AIC) is implicated in a wide range of conditions and behaviours, from bowel distension and orgasm, to cigarette craving and maternal love, to decision making and sudden insight. Its function in the re-representation of interoception offers one possible basis for its involvement in all subjective feelings. New findings suggest a fundamental role for the AIC in awareness, and thus it needs to be considered as a potential neural correlate of consciousness. – A.D. Craig

> Meditation has been shown to reduce stress and to promote health and well-being, as well as to increase compassionate behaviour towards others. It reduces distress to one's own painful experiences, going along with altered neural responses, by enhancing self-regulatory processes and decreasing emotional reactivity.

In order to investigate if meditation similarly reduces distress and neural activations associated with empathy for others' socially painful experiences, a study was done which compared trait, and state effects of long-term mindfulness (LTM) meditation practice. To do so, the researchers acquired behavioural data and neural activity measures using fMRI during an empathy for social pain task while manipulating the meditation state between two groups of LTM practitioners which were matched with a control group. The results show increased activation of the anterior insula (AI) and anterior cingulate cortex (ACC) as well as the medial PFC and temporal pole when sharing others' social suffering, both in LTM practitioners and controls. However, in LTM practitioners, who practiced mindfulness meditation just prior to observing others' social pain, left AI activation was lower and the strength of AI activation following the mindfulness meditation was negatively associated with trait compassion in LTM practitioners. The findings suggest that current mindfulness meditation could provide an adaptive mechanism in coping with distress due to the empathic sharing of others' suffering, thereby possibly enabling compassionate behaviour (Laneri *et al.*, 2017). As the Dalai Lama said, "If you want others to be happy, practice compassion. If you want to be happy, practice compassion."

In fact, a brain imaging study (Dunn *et al.*, 2008) by the researchers from University of British Columbia showed that when we donate to charity, our brain's "pleasure centre" lights up like the full moon on a clear night. Another study by the researchers from University of San Diego (cooperative behaviour cascades in human social networks [Fowler, *PNAS*]) found that acts of kindness, generosity, and cooperation are contagious and have wide impact.

> In addition, studies have shown that practicing compassion and kindness has a lot of health benefits from living longer to alleviating anxiety, to lifting depression, to strengthening immunity, etc.

A highly cited UCLA School of Medicine study found that the "right anterior dorsal insula" of meditators to be highly active while in session. What does it mean? As studied by neuroscientists from University of Wisconsin using brain imaging, this happens to be the same brain area that lights up when our "kindness and compassion" is predominant.

TPJ – HOW MEDITATION BOOSTS EQ

The TPJ is an area of the brain where the temporal and parietal lobes meet, at the posterior end of the lateral sulcus (Sylvian fissure). The TPJ incorporates information from the thalamus and the limbic system as well as from the visual, auditory, and somatosensory systems. It also integrates information both from the external environment as well as within the body and then processing it.

The fact that EQ is so important can be seen from the following statements:

- "IQ gets you hired. EQ gets you promoted." – *Time Magazine*
- In his *New York Times* international bestseller "Emotional Intelligence: Why It Matters More Than IQ," Dr. Goleman's case for "EQ over IQ" was so compelling that academic textbooks had to be rewritten in his name.
- In 2013, with the goal of mapping out the "EQ" regions of the brain, researchers from University of Illinois scanned 152 Vietnam veterans using computed tomography (CT), engaged in "emotionally intelligent" – centered activities such as (in-person) social interaction.

> In a landmark finding, the brain map imaging showed one particular region, the TPJ, to be extremely important so much so that is dubbed the EQ "command and control centre." Meditation has been shown to power up emotional intelligence.

PONS – MEDITATION ENDS INSOMNIA

Pons is an essential part of the brain located above the medulla and is a very important part of brain for the regulation and control of a number of vital functions. The pons is a structure of the brain that is vital to the autonomic, sensory, and motor functions of the human body. It acts as the bridge of the central nervous system. It contains nuclei that relay signals from the forebrain to the cerebellum, along with nuclei that deal primarily with sleep, respiration, swallowing, bladder control, hearing, equilibrium, taste, eye movement, facial expressions, facial sensation, and posture.

The brainstem (especially the pons and medulla) also plays a special role in rapid eye movement (REM) sleep; it sends signals to relax muscles essential for body posture and limb movements, so that we do not act out our dreams.

REM sleep is very important for overall well-being and especially for a knowledge worker.

- What matters most is "sleep depth," that is, quality over quantity.
- It is the deeper REM level of sleep when we detoxify blood, repair organs, heal wounds, renew cells, build muscle tissue, and so forth. We need about 2 hours REM sleep every night.

- In 2014, a team of researchers from Harvard and Stanford Universities showed that meditation, powered by the magic of neuroplasticity, builds up a big and strong sleep-cantered "pons."

To summarize, research has currently established that meditation and mindfulness practices have the following impact and increased grey matter in the following areas:

- Insula – interoception; self-awareness; empathy for emotions.
- Hippocampus – visual–spatial memory; establishing context; inhibiting amygdala and cortisol.
- PFC – executive functions; attention control.
- Reduced cortical thinning with aging in insula and PFC.
- Increased activation of left frontal regions, which lifts mood. Increased gamma-range brainwaves may be associated with integration and peace.

The key findings in layman term supports what yogic thought has been saying that the attitudes such as peace, calmness, focus, benevolence, gratitude, and forgiveness (all attributes of heartfulness) can all be learnt through meditation and awareness at any stage of one's life. It takes about 41 days for a neural pathway to be created which is why most ancient practices emphasize this number for fasting or for changing habits. Having once formed a neural pathway, practice is the key to sustain that pathway.

KEY TAKEAWAYS

Given that we have currently established the importance of meditation and its impact on almost all walks of life (life and leadership) and its importance to bring about inner alchemy, the next couple of chapters will talk of the essentials of meditation and concentration. Primarily to be mindful and be in the present moment is not that easy as mindfulness instructors make it out to be. It is a three-step process by which thoughts need to be reduced and this means that the wavering mind needs to be reined in.

1. *Withdrawal of the senses* (primarily understanding what our desires are and where they arise from, become more aware of them, and then withdraw the senses from such desires). This also calls for cleansing the subconscious mind since that is what drives desires.
2. *Concentration.* The wavering mind then needs to be made more focused. A focused mind can move mountains just as a magnifying glass that helps to focus the rays of the sun.
3. *Meditation.* It is actually something that happens by itself once the first two steps are practiced and some measures of proficiency achieved in those two steps.

Meditation is a very important tool in the arsenal of a leader and can be effectively used to train and calm the mind. The basics of meditation are dealt with in the following chapter.

8 Understanding the Basics of Meditation

The state of the mind in which there are no distracting thoughts is meditation, and there is the continuous flow of perception or thought towards one single object. There is only one mental modification or thought, whatever that thought is, and it is the flow of continuous thought of one thing like the continuous flow of water in a waterfall. Hence, meditation is the regular flow of thought with regard to the object of concentration and it follows concentration. Normally this aspect, namely concentration, which is very important to the practice of meditation is ignored or not given enough importance and as we shall see this reduces the effectiveness of meditation.

In the eightfold path of yoga (as enunciated by Patanjali, the father of the yoga system), meditation is the seventh step in the ladder and it follows concentration and withdrawal of the senses. Yama (self-restraint), niyama (observances akin to the commandments; in fact, self-restraint and observances form the 10 commandments), asana (posture), pranayama (restraint of breath), pratyahara (abstraction or withdrawal of the senses), dharana (concentration), dhyana (meditation), samadhi (superconscious state or blissful union with the Supreme Self) are the eight steps of yoga. This process of making the mind calm and without thoughts requires continuous and intense practice.

NECESSITY FOR MEDITATION

Meditation is one the easiest and best ways for attaining peace and understanding the self, as elaborated in previous chapters, and it is currently supported by scientific research and the increased interest shown by corporate executives and successful people worldwide. Through meditation, one can understand the functioning of the mind and reduce the leakage of energy by way of negative thoughts. This also helps to reduce stress and anxiety as so many studies have shown, and this has been quoted in previous chapters. An ability to control one's negative emotions and to build on the positive emotions is another great benefit and as we have seen in the chapter on leadership, most effective leaders need this as part of their arsenal. As the *Forbes* magazine put it so well, "Meditation isn't just about sitting down and emptying your mind. That's one of the biggest misconceptions. It's about self-care and learning how to focus the mind – something that business leaders need in today's hectic work environment. Incorporating meditation into one's life can help reduce stress, improve decision-making, enhance creativity and increase emotional resilience." Large corporates and businesses such as Google, Ford Motor Company, McKesson, and American Express are offering senior executives training in meditation programmes to enhance their leadership skills.

Rich Fernandez, the CEO of SIYLI and previously the Director of Executive Education and People Development at Google and a PhD in Psychology from Columbia University, said that "resilience is inner calm – the skill of mindfulness and managing your attention. Something happens when you are able to direct your awareness to the present moment – it becomes less reactive. Emotional resilience is to be aware of the emotions when you are able to notice it as they are arising. Self-awareness creates response flexibility and one is able to manage them respond better."

> Here is a fascinating story of Sally Sullenberger, which most of us must have heard of as it was made into a very successful and gripping movie. On 15 January 2009, US Airways Flight 1549 suffered an emergency landing on the Hudson River in New York. About a minute after taking off from New York's La Guardia Airport on 15 January 2009, US Airways Flight 1549 collided with one of the aviation industry's most threatening foes: a flock of geese. Ninety seconds later, Sullenberger glided the Airbus 320 with skill and composure over the George Washington Bridge and onto the sub-zero Hudson River, where it splashed down midway between Manhattan and New Jersey. There were no fatalities.

Some of the lessons that have been articulated both in articles and in the movie which are relevant to this context are:

1. *Simplicity*. In the movie, there is a scene where the flock of Canadian geese strike the plane's two engines. The result was that the engines went up in flames, and alarm bells began to sound in the cockpit. This should have reduced any normal person in the pilot's cabin into a state of panic and total inaction. Likewise, in all our lives there are times where we all face unexpected, disruptive, and at times catastrophic issues be it an accident, death, a loss of job, etc. The gears of decision-making grind to a halt, and paralysis sets in when we are beset with multiple problems. It is at these times that we react and often times not remain calm with the ability to reason and respond.
2. *Focus*. "Just Fly the Plane." There is a scene in the movie where there is a man who is training young Sully to fly. His parting words to Sully were: "Whatever happens, just fly the plane." When Sully and his co-pilot were faced with the bird strike, life hung in the balance with every passing second. Quick decisions based on years of experience was the ask of the moment. Decisions had to be made quickly. In that moment, Sully employed simplicity so beautifully. Sully decided to go into the water (despite the air traffic controllers' pleas about available runways nearby that the captain could know that he could not reach successfully). At that moment, Sully only cared about three things: altitude, air speed, and the angle of attack.
3. *Self-awareness*. People experience denial, apathy/paralysis, physical reactions, and in extreme cases, even PTSD (Post Traumatic Stress Disorders) after a disruptive event. Self-awareness involves "tuning into" oneself and seeing what he/she is experiencing, feeling, and thinking. Research has shown that being aware of what one is feeling can reduce stress. It can be measured physically through one's heart rate, blood pressure, and the release of endocrine hormones.
4. *Manage oneself before trying to manage others*. Margaret Mead once said, "courage is staying calm three seconds longer than everyone else." The standard response to crises is to cling to what is familiar and to stick diligently to established policies and procedures. The ability to manage crises and stay cool through the whole experience needs to be cultivated.

All the above lessons can be cultivated with meditation which may take many forms of heartful meditation, mindfulness, etc. It is said that if one can meditate properly for half an hour, he/she will be able to engage him/herself with peace and focus in day-to-day life for 1 week through the force of this meditation. The wandering of the mind will gradually cease through regular meditation and will gradually help remove irritability and augment one's peace of mind considerably. Research shows that 15 minutes of mindfulness-based meditation results in more rational thinking when making business decisions. Studies have also found that leaders who focus on mindfulness at work tend to have happier employees and improved morale. In addition, mindfulness meditation can help reduce chronic lower back pain and insomnia.

Meditation can be of tremendous help during current situation when one in two people are stressed out because of Covid-19-related uncertainties. At the risk of being repetitive, practising meditation has been shown to reduce anxiety, calm the amygdala, increase our ability to think creatively, and empathetically take other people's perspective. Steve Jobs, an early adaptor of meditation, described his experience: "You start to see things more clearly and be in the present more. Your mind just slows down, and you see a tremendous expanse in the moment. You see so much more than you could see before."

Hence, it makes a lot of sense for people to

- Meditate first in the morning.
- Start each meeting with a few minutes of meditation.
- Step back when they get caught in unproductive thought patterns and take a few moments to focus the mind and become self-aware.

PRACTICAL ASPECT OF MEDITATION

The mode of meditation differs according to the path adopted by a person.

(i) One who is more emotional practices meditation on a personal God like Krishna, Rama, Jesus, etc.
(ii) One who is more physical in approach meditates on the Chakras (described later) and the presiding deities.
(iii) One who is very intellectually inclined meditates on his/her own Self.
(iv) An advanced meditator who is not affected by afflictions and desires and who has a balance of the above three meditates on the Infinite – one without form.

There is no single prescription that fits all. While it is fashionable at present, especially in the West, to talk about mindfulness, it is both difficult to achieve this state continuously and also not something that suits all. Emotionally charged people may find visualization on issues, such as gratitude, kindness, love, and empathy, far more calming and effective. The choice depends on one's temperament and outlook and hence the different routes to meditate which all lead to that one state where there is a focus of the mind, a reduction in thought patterns, and a calm and steady demeanour. The first benefit is the reduction of stress, worries, etc. and it also helps one to realize his/her true nature and become a better human being which in turn helps build a better world.

The mind assumes the form of the object it cognizes which enables perception. When a person constantly meditates on any object, the mind always takes the form of the object meditated upon. When one is established in one's meditation, he starts seeing that object everywhere. The names and forms vanish. One who meditates on one's self sees his/her own Self everywhere. The world of names and forms vanishes from his/her view. He experiences the state where everything in the universe is of that one consciousness and is connected. While this may be possible only after a great deal of time and may not be suitable for everybody, even a little bit of meditation helps in calming the mind and setting one on the path of peace and tranquillity with all its attendant benefits of better health, reduced stress, better rational thinking, and so on as described in the earlier chapters.

Unless the mind is set free and casts away all desires, cravings, worries, delusion, pride, lust, attachment, likes, and dislikes, it cannot enter into the domain of peace. A glutton or a sensualist, a dullard or a lazy man, cannot achieve a tranquil mind. No amount of material wealth and comforts can help one achieve peace as we have been seeing with cases of Hollywood celebrities and business magnates resorting to drugs and other stimulants to transcend the mind. One who has controlled the tongue and other organs, who eats, drinks, and sleeps in moderation, and who has destroyed selfishness, lust, greed, and anger can practise meditation and attain success.

If there is tossing of mind and mental turbulence, one cannot enjoy peace of mind and this calls for some amount of meditation. All mental activities are called as Rajas. Mental activity and desires coexist in the mind. If one really wants to destroy this mental turbulence (which is the root cause of diseases, worry, tension, stress, etc.), then one must control desires and cravings within limits through dispassion and self-surrender to a larger purpose. It is very similar to green/fresh wood not catching fire, however one tries much to burn it, but if one applies fire to a piece of dried wood it will burn immediately. Similar is the case with those whose mind is not purified, meditation or being in the moment or mindfulness will not happen. The mind must first be purified with service, charity, chanting, pranayama, breath control, etc. which can then be stilled and peace ensues. The mind is often compared with a garden where one can cultivate good flowers and fruits in a garden by ploughing and manuring the land, by removing the weeds and thorns, and by watering the plants and trees. Similarly, one can also cultivate the flower of meditation and stillness in the garden of one's mind by removing the impurities of the mind, such as lust, anger, greed, delusion, pride, etc., and watering it with good positive thoughts. Just as weeds and thorns grow in the rainy season and disappear in summer, so also the modifications of the mind manifest on the surface of the conscious mind, then disappear, and assume a subtle seed state in the form of impressions. As soon as there is a shower, the seeds again germinate and sprout out. Even so, the impressions again sprout through internal or external stimulus. This is why most mindfulness is temporary and deals only with the surface impressions. When the garden is clean and when there are no weeds and thorns one can get good fruits. Similarly, when the mind is pure and is free from emotions such as lust, anger, greed, jealousy etc., one can have the fruit of good, deep meditation. Therefore, it is imperative to cleanse the mind of its impurities first, whereby meditation becomes natural and continuous.

ERRORS IN MEDITATION

A mixture of drowsiness and sleepiness is often mistaken for deep meditation. That is a fallacy. The mind appears to be established in concentration and free from distraction which is a mistake. Deep sleep state is mistaken by many for meditation. Meditation is a positive, real state when the mind passes into a calm state of equanimity. Diet and a positive mindset play an important part in achieving equanimity.

INSTRUCTIONS ON MEDITATION

Regularity in meditation is a sine qua non for success. One will have to purify the sensuous mind through concentration, self-reflection, and meditation on an object both externally or internally. The mind must be filled with positive thoughts that help to drive away the negative thoughts. A positive thought drives off a negative one, courage drives off fear, love destroys hatred, unity annihilates separateness, and magnanimity destroys jealousy. Generosity drives away miserliness and greed. This helps in stilling the mind and also conserving energy which can then be used to focus on the work at hand.

REACTION IN MEDITATION

Similar to when one who begins to sweep a closed room after a length of time, various kinds of dirt come out from the corners of the room. Similarly during meditation various kinds of impurities float about on the surface of the mind. Efforts are needed to be self-aware which is facilitated by solitude and silence and needs to be weeded out. Rather than making any violent efforts to control the mind, just observing the thoughts as they float around (described as mindfulness or better described as awareness) helps to quieten the mind.

EXERCISES IN MEDITATION (AS ADVOCATED BY SRI SWAMI SIVANANDA OF RISHIKESH)

- Place a picture of any God (who appeals to you – Krishna, Shiva, Jesus, etc.) in front of you. Sit in a comfortable position either on the chair or on the ground on a blanket. Concentrate gently with open eyes on the picture till tears trickle down your cheeks. Rotate the mind on the various other limbs of His body, and the spiritual aura that is emanating. Then close the eyes and try to visualize the picture. Repeat the same process again and again.
- Another kind of meditation is to sit comfortably as described earlier with eyes closed and meditate on the effulgence in the sun, or the splendour in the moon or the glory in the stars or of anything in nature that is appealing.
- Another process is to meditate on the magnanimity of the ocean and its infinite nature. Then compare the ocean with the infinite Brahman, and the waves, foams, and icebergs to the various names and forms. Identify yourself with the ocean. Become silent and expand. One gets a sense of completeness and peace as he/she goes through this meditation.
- There is a living universal Power that underlies all these names and forms. Meditate on this Power that is formless. This will terminate in the realization of the absolute formless consciousness eventually.
- In a comfortable sitting posture, with eyes closed gaze steadily on the formless air only. Concentrate on the air. Meditate on the all-pervading nature of the air. This leads to the realization of the nameless and formless being, the one living Truth and a very effective way to control the mind.
- Concentrate and meditate on the expansive blue sky. The mind will cease thinking of finite forms, forget the worries and stresses, and slowly begin to melt in the ocean of peace, as it is deprived of its contents. The mind will become subtler and subtler.
- Another method is to keep a picture of OM in front of you and concentrate gently on this picture with open eyes till tears flow profusely. Associate the ideas of eternity, infinity, immortality, etc., when you think of OM. The humming of bees, the sweet notes of the nightingale, the seven notes in music, and all other sounds are emanations from this soundless sound "OM" which forever reverberates in the universe and is the creative force of nature. In a state of mental stillness, one can hear this sound within oneself.
- In a comfortable sitting posture, just watch the flow of breath. Breathe in with the silent sound "So" and breathe out with the silent chant of "Ham." When the mind is still, one can actually hear that while breathing this sound is made automatically without any effort. One is unconsciously repeating Soham 21,600 times daily at the rate of 15 Soham per minute. Send out waves of love and gratitude to the universe and to your loved ones. These will impact one's mind very positively.

KEY TAKEAWAY

This chapter dealt with practices in meditation – the do's and the don'ts. Some exercises were also suggested. While meditation and mindfulness (mindfulness practices is one of the tools used to meditate) are very important, they are far more effective if one learns to focus the mind for which concentration practices are a very important tool. The following chapter explains concentration in detail along with suggesting some exercises that help one to concentrate better.

9 Meditation Happens While Concentration can be Practised

Concentration is one-pointedness of the mind, the ability to hold all thoughts to one object without wavering. The perfection of concentration leads to meditation which is the distinction-less state of subject and the object, i.e. the meditator and the object of meditation. In the highest state of meditation, awareness is non-dual. In the state of concentration, the mind is not aware of any other object other than the object that is focused on. Concentration is important because the mind is like sunlight whose rays are diffused but if focused by a magnifying glass on a single point the rays have the power to burn the object or create a fire. Similarly, a focused mind can do wonders because it unlocks a source of great power, most of which we are unaware about as concentrated thought also has great power. It has the power of heightened perception and the ability to achieve great things including unimaginable amounts of work. This is a very important tool to be cultivated by leaders, professionals, and students alike. As an aside, *Mantras* (from *Manas Trayate* in Sanskrit, meaning helping to provide direction to the mind) are great tools to help in bringing about focus through the medium of subtle sound.

Work done with a concentrated mind becomes more enjoyable as described by Daniel Goleman (2013) in his book *Focus*. In this book, he described how focus and attention make life interesting and worth living and showed how one can be more focused in every area of life including work, relationships, and one's own attitudes towards life.

A person with a concentrated mind can do all kinds of work with great efficiency, an attribute that is especially useful for the knowledge worker.

Hence it is imperative that knowledge workers are trained in developing a concentrated mind. Recent research (as mentioned earlier) pointed to the neuroplasticity of the mind which can be trained with discipline and practices to become more focused and concentrated. Currently, there is ample research to show the benefits of a concentrated mind on health parameters (Raub, 2002). In fact, current research in neurology says that over 60–70% of all illnesses are related to mind in nature. Yoga has been saying this all along that all diseases are products of the unconscious mind, and of the impressions that are stored in the Chitta (loosely defined as the subconscious). A concentrated mind can be used in conjunction with modern medicines and Ayurveda (the traditional Indian system of medicine which is the science of longevity) to speed-up the cure for diseases and also to find a cure for the so-called incurable diseases.

> Yoga teaches us to cure the things that need not be endured, and to endure the things that cannot be cured. – B.K.S. Iyengar

Concentration is spoken of in the Katha Upanishad as, "The firm control of the senses and the mind is the yoga of concentration. One must be ever watchful for this yoga is difficult to acquire and easy to lose". Unfortunately in modern education the way to train one's mind and make it more concentrated is not formally taught. As we grow older, the mind becomes more and more dissipated as tensions and worries mount. This results in increasing loss of mental ability, wrong decisions, ineffective management, and fading memory. Developing concentration is not a superficial practice. It involves diving deep into the inner dimensions of the mind and consciousness.

Concentration is an important means of reducing stress. Most of the time the dissipated mind is not at rest and even without our conscious knowledge it is active with thoughts and emotions at a subconscious level. While we are aware of one train of thought, inputs are being constantly received, processed, and filtered by the other sense organs, namely the brain and the mind. Hence it is very difficult to be completely concentrated. The science of Yoga (described by Patanjali) has outlined a systematic process to maintain mental discipline. He has outlined the eightfold path, starting with prescriptions of do's and don'ts (the 10 commandments) which help to control and pacify the sense organs and organs of action. Thereafter, the next six steps are asana physical exercises (to ensure a healthy body), pranayama (to control the life force energy through the breath), pratyahara (the withdrawal of the senses so that the mind is no more excited just as a tortoise withdraws into itself), dharana (which is concentration), dhyana (meditation), (which is not by conscious effort but happens of its own accord once the mind is calm), and finally samadhi, which is a more intense form of meditation where the subject–object distinction is dissolved and where one rests in pure unfettered consciousness.

For the purposes of this discussion, we will focus on just four of the six steps, namely yoga asana (popularly referred to as yoga), pranayama (right and conscious breathing), pratyahara (control of the senses), and dharana (concentration).

Yoga is extremely effective for ensuring that all parts of the body are kept healthy. This is done through specific postures, synchronization, and concentration of the mind and breath to the activity and awareness to the subtle effects of the posture. This is not just a physical exercise but has a deep positive impact on the internal organs especially the endocrine system.

Pranayama is breath with awareness. Although breathing normally happens unconsciously, it is far more beneficial if one takes conscious control of the process. The unconscious nervous system control of the breath originates in the medulla oblongata of the brainstem, a region known as the primitive brain. The conscious control of the breath is done by the more evolved areas of the brain in the cerebral cortex. During conscious control of the breath, the cerebral cortex bypasses the respiratory centre in the brainstem. This has an emotionally calming effect as the PFC areas of the brain are what control emotions consciously. This is one of the most effective methods of quietening a tense mind. Just becoming aware of the breath is enough as it engages the PFC and stimulates the more evolved areas of the brain. Yogic deep diaphragmatic breathing is therefore highly recommended. There are several other techniques each of which has a unique function in balancing the constituents of the physical body by impacting specific areas of the subtle body.

Pratyahara is the process of disconnecting the mind from the sense organs and this is done by consciously withdrawing the mind from the external sensory organs. This calls for shutting out the link between the sense objects of the external world and the organs of knowledge (sense organs). In spite of this, there could be disturbances as old memories surface and the chattering of the mind continues internally. However, concentration will not be possible unless some form of withdrawal takes place and this is usually done by going to a quiet place where there are no distractions from the five senses, namely smell, taste, form, touch, and sound.

Concentration is stilling in the mind and focusing on one object or thought with intensity and regularity. Over time the mind becomes completely stilled and can be done in many ways. The objects of concentration can be seen or located internally or externally depending on the comfort of the person. Concentration can also be done in the different parts of the body (or the psychic centres, described later, and which has extraordinary benefits) or on the breath itself. One can choose any symbol, however the symbol must have meaning to the practitioner and the mind must be drawn to the symbol and integrate effortlessly with it.

Mindfulness practice in reality is not easy. As research shows that even the superficial mindfulness that is widely practised is so beneficial. The benefits would be far greater if only the mind is a little more concentrated. Normally when one tries to bring the awareness to the present moment, it lasts for a few seconds and then it starts wandering or the mind just blanks out. There is great effort required in bringing it back repeatedly. Instead of mindfulness, we end up with a constant struggle to bring the mind back to the practice. It is far better to spend some time in stilling the mind through concentration practices and then mindfulness will become a habit by itself. This is the reason why some symbol which has particular meaning is first used and this acts as a point to focus our attention. This aspect has been elaborated later in this chapter.

Pranayama and withdrawal from sensual objects will pave a long way in achieving rapid success in concentration. Concentration is the sixth step in the yogic ladder. There can be no concentration without something upon which the mind may rest. A definite purpose, interest, and attention will bring success in concentration and for this the senses have to be controlled first as they draw one out and perturb his/her peace of mind. If the mind is restless, no progress can be made and for this first the ceaseless flow of thoughts and the resultant emotions need to be kept in check. Patience, persistence, and regularity are also required.

Everybody possesses some ability to concentrate. But for a leader, concentration should be developed to a very high degree. A man with an appreciable degree of concentration has more earning capacity and turns out more work in a shorter time. A person whose mind is filled with passion and all sorts of desires can hardly concentrate on any object.

Concentration enables doing work with greater efficiency and helps to purify and calms the surging emotions, strengthens the current of thought, and clarifies ideas. The mind should be trained to concentrate on gross objects in the beginning, and later on one can successfully concentrate on subtle objects and abstract ideas. Regularity in the practice is the key to success.

ATTENTION AND THE PRACTICE OF CONCENTRATION

Concentration is easy and deep if all distractions are removed. This also needs to be practised for a few minutes daily by fixing the mind on an object either externally or internally which helps the mind get focused and attention spans become deep and sharp. This is a vital ability for anyone who deals with knowledge work and where the mind needs to be applied. This also helps the mind to focus and reduces negative emotions like worry and stress as proved in many research studies.

Attention is steady application of the mind and focusing of consciousness on some chosen object. Through attention, one can develop his/her mental ability. Attention also improves perception of people and objects which aids memory. Improving attention also helps to improve will power when such attention is guided inwards and one introspects on a subject.

SOME EXERCISES IN CONCENTRATION

(i) Look at some playing cards. Immediately after the exposure, describe the forms you have seen. Give the number, name, etc., such as king of clubs, 10 of spades, queen of diamonds, and jack of hearts.

(ii) Close a book after reading two or three pages. Try and recall what one has read and recall the details of what you have read. Allow the mind to associate, classify, group, combine, and compare.

(iii) Concentrate on the sound of a clock ticking or watch one's own breath. Whenever the mind wanders, bring it back. Check how long it rests on the chosen stimulus – sound/breath.

(iv) Concentrate on a candle flame kept in front of you. After a few minutes, close your eyes and try to visualize the flame internally. Check how long the flame lasts within.

A recent study of personality and reasoning in 800 senior managers by Deloitte explored the relationship between personality factors, reasoning abilities, and the speed at which individuals moved into senior management positions in organizations. The study showed that "high flyers" are elevated on many indicators of effective social functioning, as well as on breadth and creativity of thinking. It also showed the importance of building "soft skills" in organizations. Some of these soft skills in people included less vulnerability to stress and extrovertedness, openness to one's own feelings, and higher emotional self-awareness similar to overall conscientiousness.

All these factors are traits that can be developed through strengthening the mind through concentration, meditation, and positive visualization exercises.

KEY TAKEAWAY

A concentrated mind is ready to meditate. Conversely, meditation and mindfulness are hardly possible if the rays of the mind are diffused. This chapter looked at concentration in some detail and a few exercises in improving concentration skills were also suggested. The following chapter discusses about physical postures and breath control as a prelude to concentration as without physical health concentration is extremely difficult. Besides, it is easier to control the mind through the breath, rather than directly. This is dealt with in detail in the following chapter.

10 Starting with Physical Postures and Breath Control

Patanjali wrote down the principles of yoga practice in the "Yoga Sutras" (aphorisms). He named only the meditation posture as "asana" and the physical postures as "Yoga Vyayam." However, in common usage the dynamic yoga exercises also became asanas. Asana is the Sanskrit word for a physical posture. Many asanas were derived from the natural movements and positions of animals and carry the names of animals such as "cat," "deer," "tiger," and "hare." These postures make use of examples from nature on how to help oneself. Asanas have a far-reaching effect upon body and mind. Animals instinctively used these movements and positions because of their natural benefits. These effects are attained through the practice of the asanas, for example, Marjari (The Cat) for stretching the body and the spine, Bhujangasana (The Cobra) for the release of aggression and emotions, and Shashankasana (The Hare) for relaxation.

Asanas are beneficial for the muscles, joints, cardiovascular system, nervous system, and lymphatic system, as well as the mind, psyche, and chakras (energy centres). They are psychosomatic exercises, which strengthen and balance the entire nervous system and harmonize and stabilize the practitioner's state of mind. The effects of these exercises are freedom from disease and clarity of mind. They are not only physical postures and exercise but they also combine physical postures with awareness and breath.

Deep breathing and periods of relaxation are included at the beginning and end of each exercise and groups of exercise which have to be done in such a manner that there is a counter pose for each pose. Physical and mental relaxation are prerequisites for the correct performance of all yoga exercises and it is only in this way that the effects of the asanas completely unfold.

The breath plays an important role in the asanas. With coordination of breath and movement, the yoga practice becomes harmonious, the breath deepens of its own accord, and the body's circulation and metabolism are stimulated. Use of the breath greatly enhances muscle relaxation by concentrating on tense areas of the body and consciously relaxing those parts with each exhalation.

Seven out of ten people breathe wrongly. A simple exercise will prove it out. Just place your hands (where) when you breathe in and see what happens to the abdomen. It should be like a baby's breath, meaning it should expand when breath is taken in and contract when the breath goes out. But quite the opposite happens to most people and this is the root cause of many illnesses. Also most people breathe very shallow. Correct breathing is fundamental for the body's optimum metabolic function. With regular practice, the Full Yoga Breath becomes the habitual and natural way of breathing. Slower and deeper breaths improve circulation, nerve function, and whole physical condition. They also develop a calm, clear mind.

IMPORTANT PRINCIPLES FOR PRACTICE OF THE ASANAS

1. Asanas are always performed in coordination with the breath:
   - Movements that expand the chest and abdominal cavity are always connected with the inhalation.
   - Movements that narrow the chest and abdominal cavity are always connected with the exhalation.
2. In the initial stages of practice, the asanas are performed once or twice without holding, so that the movement of the body and the breath are synchronized. In this way, it is clearly established with which movement to inhale or exhale. This type of practice calms the nervous system, stimulates the glands, increases the capacity of the breath, and frees one from physical and mental stress. The mind becomes relaxed, calm, and clear.
3. Only after this preliminary practice should an asana be held for a longer time, breathing normally. During practice, concentration is directed to the specific part of the body on which the exercise is working. The breath consciousness is also directed to this region of the body.
4. After practicing a posture, a counter pose or equalizing posture is carried out. For example, when one part of the body is flexed or contracted, then in the following asana it is extended or stretched.

SOME OF THE HEALTH BENEFITS FROM THE REGULAR PRACTICE OF ASANAS

- Flexibility of the spine is increased.
- Immune system is strengthened.
- Muscles are relaxed and they receive a plentiful supply of blood.
- The joints become more mobile.
- Metabolism is stimulated.
- Clear and fresh skin.
- The lymphatic system is strengthened.
- Organ and glandular activity is stimulated and regulated.
- Circulation and blood pressure are normalized and stabilized.
- The nervous system remains calm and strengthened.

PRANA AND PRANAYAMA

What is Prana?

Prana is the sum total of all energy that is manifest in the universe and is the sum total of all the forces in nature. All physical and mental forces fall under the category "prana." Whatever moves or works or has life is, but an expression or manifestation of that life, force. The prana is related to mind and through mind to will, through will to the individual soul, and through soul to the Supreme Being. The commonly known "power of personality" is being successful in life and being more influential than others, which is due to the power of this prana and is most often manipulated unconsciously. This work of prana is seen in the systolic and diastolic actions of the heart, when it pumps the blood into arteries in the action of inspiration and expiration during the course of breathing; in the digestion of food; in the excretion of urine and faecal matter; in the manufacture of semen, chyle, chyme, gastric juice, bile, intestinal juice, saliva; in closing and opening of the eyelids, in walking, playing, running, talking, thinking, reasoning, feeling, and willing. Prana is the link between the mind and the physical body. When the slender thread-link prana is cut off, death takes place (Swami Sivananda).

By controlling the act of breathing, one can efficiently control all the various motions in the body and the different nerve currents that are running through the body. Body, mind, and soul can easily and quickly be controlled and developed. Through pranayama, one can also control his/her circumstances and character. The breath, directed by thought under the control of the will, is a vitalizing, regenerating force that one can utilize consciously for self-development and also for healing many incurable diseases in his/her system.

Fourth Step in Patanjali's Yoga after Asana (Exercises) is Pranayama (or Breath Control)

Pranayama is the conscious and deliberate control and regulation of the breath (prana means life energy breath and ayam means to control and to regulate). So in reality it is not control of breath but control of life force energy through the regulation of the breath. With each breath we absorb not only oxygen, but also prana. Prana is cosmic energy, that is, the power in the Universe which creates, preserves, and changes. It is the basic element of life and consciousness. Prana is also found in food, therefore it is very important to have a healthy and wholesome vegetarian diet. Most importantly prana is used up in our thoughts, so it is very important to regulate our thoughts, especially negative thoughts that consume a disproportionate amount of life force energy.

The conscious guidance of prana in the body gives rise to an increase in vitality, physical detoxification, and improved immunity, as well as to the attainment of inner peace, relaxation, and mental clarity.

In yogic thought, it is said that the life span of every person is determined by the number of breaths and one can increase his/her life span by reducing the number of breaths that he/she takes per minute. It is no coincidence that the tortoise takes only 1 or 2 breaths per minute and lives up to 500 years or more.

Effects of Pranayama

Conscious practice of pranayama has a number of health benefits both physically and mentally, which are borne out by scientific research. These are well documented but are not universally accepted.

Physical effects

- Preservation of the body's health
- Purification of the blood
- Improvement in the absorption of oxygen
- Strengthening the lungs and heart
- Regulation of blood pressure
- Regulation of the nervous system
- Increasing resistance to infection.

Mental effects

- Elimination of stress, nervousness, and depression
- Quietening of thoughts and emotions.

Spiritual effects

- Deepening of meditation and expansion of consciousness.

Pranayama is an exact science and is the fourth step of yoga. Regulation of breath or the control of prana is the stoppage of inhalation and exhalation. Breath is the external manifestation of prana, and it is through breathing one is able to control this vital force. It is the link between the physical body and the mind. Trying to directly control the mind is often difficult and unsuccessful. Controlling the mind through the regulation of the breath is far easier. It is the vibrations of prana or the vital energy that moves the mind (when one is sick, the mind becomes dull as there is very little prana or energy and that flow is disturbed). The process by which the prana is controlled by regulation of external breath is termed pranayama. Similar to a goldsmith who removes the impurities of gold by heating it in the hot furnace by strongly blowing the blow pipe, the impurities of the body can be removed by practising pranayama. The chief aim of pranayama is to unite the prana air with the apana air (described earlier) and take the united prana–apana air slowly towards the head.

Seat of Prana

The seat of prana is the heart and it assumes four forms, namely mind, intellect, memory, and ego, according to the different functions it performs. Likewise, though prana is one, it assumes five forms, namely (1) prana, (2) apana, (3) samana, (4) udana, and (5) vyana, according to the different functions it perform. It is the same Maha prana that performs various physiological processes like digestion, respiration, etc. and the prana is given different names depending on the function it performs. Practising prana involves inhaling it from outside, filling the stomach with it, and focusing it at the centre in the mind, in the middle of the navel, at the tip of the nose, and at the toes. This helps to remove diseases. Especially in this Covid-19 situation, it helps to strengthen the respiratory system in a physical sense and in a more subtle way fills one with the energy to strengthen the immune system and fight diseases.

THE LUNGS

The organs of respiration consist of two lungs, one on either side of the chest and the air passages that lead to them and they are located in the upper thoracic cavity of the chest, one on each side of the median line. They are separated from each other by the heart, the greater blood vessels, and the larger air tubes. The lungs are spongy and porous and their tissues are very elastic which contain innumerable air sacs that contain air. They are covered by a delicate serous membrane called the pleura that contains serous fluid to prevent friction of the lungs during the act of breathing. Each lung consists of an apex and a base. It is the base that gets inflamed in pneumonia. The apex of the lung which does not get proper supply of oxygen gets affected by tubercle bacilli (TB) and similar diseases. By the practice of Kapalabhati and Bhastrika Pranayama and deep breathing exercises, the lungs get good supply of oxygen which helps prevent many diseases of the lungs.

Appendix 1 describes some simple physical postures and Appendix 2 gives some important pranayama exercises. While the exercises seem simple, they are subtle exercises (*sookshma kriya* in Sanskrit) and they help to retain the flexibility of the body besides ensuring that toxins do not build up. This is the root cause of pains and aches. The breathing exercises are simple and very effective and need to be done in the order in which they are indicated with concentration and awareness. Readers are cautioned that ideally this should be initially practiced under the guidance of a trained expert and this should be avoided if one is unsure or has any medical condition. This has been described here only by way of information and education.

KEY TAKEAWAY

This chapter outlined some simple physical postures and breath control as a prelude to concentration as without physical health concentration is extremely difficult. Besides it is easier to control the mind through the breath than directly. This is dealt with in some detail in this chapter. The following chapter discusses some practices that have not been explored/validated yet by any current scientific research but have been in vogue with great results for centuries in yogic practice.

11 Beyond Current Scientific Knowledge

Our physical body has a circuit network made up of arteries, veins, nerves, and the organs. Similarly there is a subtle body of energy (energy body) that cannot be seen and touched where all life force energy or prana flows. This circuit network in the subtle body is made up of chakras and nadis through which life force energy or prana flows. It is believed that the human body actually has 109 chakras (energy centres), but among those nine centres are important, and even among those nine, seven chakras are of primary importance. Each centre is associated with different elements and emotions. Out of these, there are three main nadis – Sushumna (runs through the spinal cord), Ida (runs through left nostril), and Pingala (runs through right nostril).

The literal meaning of chakra is wheel or circle. Chakras correspond to nerve centres or nerve plexus in the gross body and are energy centres or energy reservoirs. All these centres are connected with each other through nadis or channels of metaphysical energy through which life force (prana) flows. We have already seen the importance of prana (energy) in Chapter 10 on Pranayama, and the channels through which this energy flows is called a nadi in yoga parlance. Of course, science does not speak of nadis but just because one cannot see with the eye he/she does not obviate its existence. Similar to science that currently accepts the benefits of pranayama and deep breathing, it is a matter of time before the understanding of the nadis becomes more than what it is today. For meditators, a subtle mind can feel and probably see the flow of such energy, based on which the sages of yore have described the existence and functioning of the nadis and chakras.

NADIS

Nadis are astral tubes made up of astral matter which carry pranic currents. They do not refer to the nerves and are 72,000 in number. Ida, Pingala, and Sushumna are the important ones of which Sushumna is the most important.

IDA AND PINGALA

There are two nerve currents or nadis, one on either side of the spinal column. The left one is called Ida and the right is known as Pingala. Some consider these as the right and the left sympathetic cords (Pingala as the parasympathetic nervous system and Ida as the sympathetic nervous system) but they are subtle tubes that carry prana. Ida is cooling and flows through the left nostril while Pingala is heating and flows through the right nostril.

The breath alternates through each of the nostrils (left nostril and right nostril) for approximately one-and-a-half hour each and this is a sign of good health. One can check this by just placing a finger below

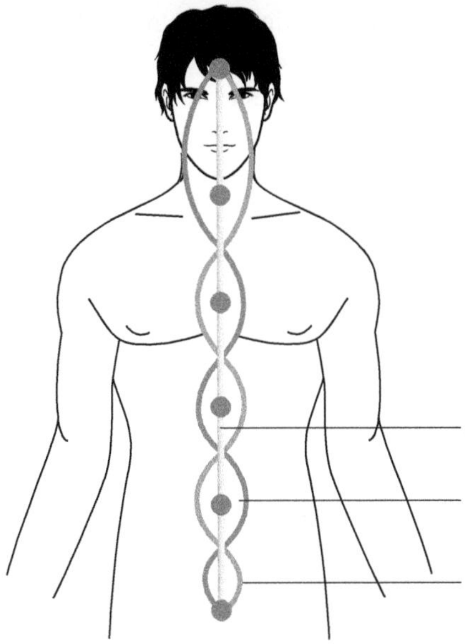

the nostril and checking from which nostril the air is coming out through. It will be found that only one nostril is dominant at any one time for most people. It is only at very specific times during the day (morning, noon and evening called sandhya or transition times) that both nostrils are active together or in the case of advanced yogis. When this flow is disturbed, it is an early indication of disturbances in the energy body which will translate into a physical ailment after a period of time. Based on this, the traditional practitioners of siddha and other forms of medicine determine the kinds of ailments that one is susceptible to.

SUSHUMNA

Sushumna is the most important of all the nadis (with a link to the central nervous system) and is generally the one activated by yogis. However, we will not go into this in great detail as that is not the purpose of this book.

SIGNIFICANCE OF THE CHAKRAS

Each chakra is symbolized as a lotus with differing numbers of petals. The lotus is a symbol of discrimination and dispassion (it does not get affected by the filth around it even if it grows in dirty waters). The petals symbolize the energy flows (with links to the nerves in the physical body) that are linked to each energy vortex. For the sake of simplicity, we will not go into detail on the symbolization of the petals but just look at the chakras overall so as to enable us to do a simple but very effective meditation which has been described in Chapter 11.

There are over 72,000 nadis in the human body of which the three principal ones as mentioned earlier are the Ida (lunar energy starting at the left of the body near the tail bone), Pingala (solar energy on the right near the tail bone), and the Sushumna (the central channel going straight up from the base of the tail bone to the pineal gland). The Ida and the Pingala nadis criss-cross at four major centres (points at which the Ida, Pingala, and Sushumna meet) and these areas are called the chakras or the "wheels," and these are energy vortexes that are roughly supposed to correspond to the "plexuses" in the physical body (see figure above).

The moon symbolizes the mind with its changeable feelings, whereas the sun represents the intellect. Similar to our emotions and thoughts that change constantly, the moon is also constantly changing its form. The intellect, however, is a stable and constant principle like the sun. Only when harmony and balance prevail between the moon and sun systems (the female and the male attributes within us), we are healthy and capable of developing further mentally and spiritually.

The breath is the key to activating and harmonizing the nadis. When we breathe through the left nostril, we activate the Ida nadi that cools, quietens, and refreshes body and mind. The Pingala nadi is influenced by breathing through the right nostril and this has a warming and activating influence. A simple experiment on oneself will prove the point. When one is very agitated in the mind, just close the right nostril, and breathe through the left nostril for about 6–8 minutes. Observe the effect the breath has on the mind and nerves. This is a very useful tool to employ when one is agitated or before one goes into a stress situation.

Ida and Pingala begin in the brain at approximately the level of the pituitary gland and have an effect on the right and left sides of the brain, respectively.

Chakras are centres of spiritual energy. They are located in the astral/mental body, and they have corresponding centres in the physical body and cannot be seen by the naked eyes. Roughly, they correspond to certain plexuses in the physical body. There are seven important chakras. They are:

(i) Root chakra at the anus/tip of the tail bone (coccygeal plexus)
(ii) At the genital organ, 6 inches above the tail bone (prostatic plexus/sacral plexus)
(iii) At the navel (solar plexus)
(iv) At the heart (cardiac/brachial/thoracic plexus)
(v) At the throat (laryngeal/cervical)
(vi) At the space between the two eyebrows (cavernous plexus/the medulla oblongata)
(vii) At the top of the head, top of the cranium.

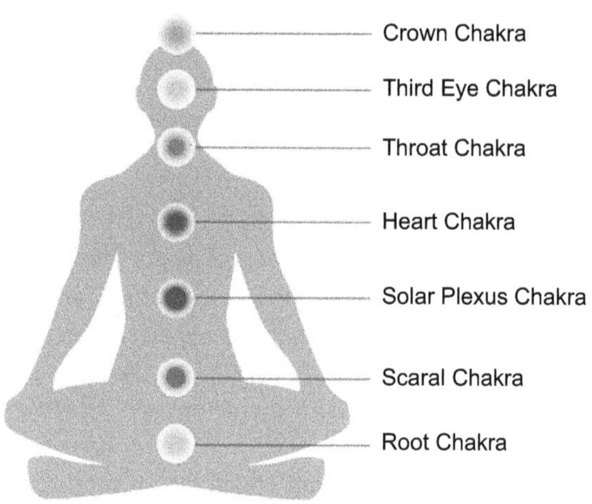

Mindful breathing at these points directs the flow of prana here and they have a corresponding benefit in the physical plexus as well.

Each of the chakras or wheels at the plexus points in the nadis is huge energy vortex that if tapped and channelized can energize the body parts corresponding to that plexus and the associated endocrine gland. The chakras are energy.

Science has recently started research in some of these aspects. Hopefully, we will get a better scientific understanding as the interest in this aspect of our being and consciousness gets more exposure and acceptance. Currently, neuroscience is moving in that direction as it still has been unable to explain "why" the various parts of the brain and the nervous system work the way they do. Till such time, it may be better to experiment oneself and understand from direct experience the benefits of meditating at these energy points and the effect of meditation on one's system and life. Consciousness of the world is moving in that direction, and as one practices more one gets intuitive knowledge.

KEY TAKEAWAY

This chapter discussed chakras (energy vortexes) and nadis (channels for life force energy) in a way as simple as possible. While there are far more practices than what is described here, this chapter essentially introduces the reader to some of these concepts. A simple way to effectively use these chakras to meditate with great effect is described in Appendix 3 when a simple meditation exercise is prescribed. It would be useful to memorize these chakras and locate them in one's body. The following chapter will look at the 4D practice which is the foundation for the deeper meditation practices that are described later.

12 The 4D Practice

Focus and inner mastery cannot come from an emotional mind.

For him who has conquered the mind, the mind is the best of friends; but for one who has failed to do so, his mind will remain the greatest enemy. – *Bhagavad Gita*

An uncontrolled mind has the potential to mess up a person's life due to its following characteristics:

1. It is full of likes and dislikes.
2. It has the tendency to slip into the past or the future.
3. It generates endless desires.
4. It develops attachment to objects and beings.

The mind comprises impulses, feelings, emotions, likes, and dislikes. If we are not in control of the mind, we will be controlled by the mind, having a life full of endless stress.

In the normal course, people live their lives in the past or in the future and are hardly ever in the present which is the only reality. They are either worried about the past or anxious about the future.

Focus of the mind and mindfulness can be obtained with a conscious practice of what is described as the 4D's – discrimination, dispassion (detachment), discipline, and desire (deep desire of a well-defined purpose). The 4D practice can be developed by ridding ourselves of the burden of past actions and thoughts and limiting beliefs through meditation on the body, breath, the mind itself, and the specific energy centres that were outlined in the previous chapter.

You can only train three things: your craft, your body, and your mind. – Michael Gervais

DISCRIMINATION (A DISCRIMINATING MIND; THE FIRST D)

As human beings, we all possess this wonderful tool called the discriminating consciousness or our intellect. Most people react emotionally with the mind rather than think things with the help of the intellect. It is this aspect of consciousness that determines our likes and dislikes, separates subject from object, analyses problems, and discriminates between right and wrong. The discriminative faculty (the ability to decide between right and wrong, good and bad, etc.) is normally attributed to the Buddhi or the intellect. A strong intellect can help in controlling a wavering mind and take decisions that are informed and based on facts and not mere emotions. The intellect is not only the power of discretion and judgement but also the right of perception and comprehension, rationality, wisdom, and mindfulness, all working together to keep us attuned to the world around us and deal with it wisely, appropriately, and effectively. If one wishes to take good decisions, the intellect must be strengthened and used. A strong intellect which is under control is a big asset in both material and spiritual life.

Buddhi – The Individual Intellect

The Buddhi (intellect) manifests with the diversification of the ego when the identity of the individual self, distinguishes itself from every other being in this universe. The moment an individual human exists the potential of the intellect is manifest, something that does not exist in other forms of life and that distinguishes human beings from other life forms. However, the intellect is only a possibility and a potential which needs to be developed. The name "Buddhi" comes from the same Sanskrit root as "Buddha" – from "budh" meaning "to know."

This then gives enormous freedom to the process of creation – the freedom to remain as a two-legged animal or to become a human being. This is determined by the use of the intellect – the reasoning mind. In Indian spiritual thought, the Buddhi or the intellect actually comes directly from the Mahat – the cosmic mind and is actually our own little piece of the cosmic or divine mind present only in human beings. This also means that we are the only being who can exercise our intellect and manifest free will. While our present is determined by our past actions, all of us have the capability of exercising the intellect and changing our destinies based on the possibilities that we currently have. However it cannot manifest without the presence of the ego, the sense of being an individual.

Prana manifests through Buddhi as the power of discrimination. This is the power to distinguish truth from falsehood. When the prana is low or deranged, then discrimination is lacking in the individual. This manifests as low energy levels and no desire to do anything much. Conversely, if we are full of prana or energy we are like a bubbly fountain and if channelized properly we can achieve whatever we set out to achieve.

Intellect or intellectual function is the only function of Buddhi, however it operates at three levels:

(1) On its highest level, it is the power of conscious discrimination, which is feeling, caring, and sensitive (called Sattva in Sanskrit). Here the intellect is not only concerned with oneself but also in understanding the interconnectedness of the universe. This reflects in empathy, and caring, and (–) is something which is so much required in the present world. This is the domain of purity in the intellect and is the aspect that dominates in a developed human being. Leaders who are effective exhibit this Sattvic (purity) trait to a large degree. Here is a lovely anecdote from the tennis star Vijay Amritraj which he narrated, in one his interviews. A nephew of his went to borrow ₹. 10,000 as loan from an uncle, promising to return it in 6 months. He needed it apparently to fund his education. The uncle who was not very well off financially told him that he would not loan him ₹. 10,000 but would gift him the same under the condition that when he was able to, he would do a similar gesture and help someone else in need. In Balbhojan the NGO that I am a co-founder of, and which focuses on helping children in need with their education, we have the same philosophy. Educational assistance will be granted to the deserving on the condition that they help someone else not in the distant future but in the present. It could be as simple as helping someone in a lower class with their mathematics or science tuition. This gives borrowers and recipients a sense of self-worth and self-esteem and also inculcates compassion and a sense of service in them. Learning to serve without motive is also intelligence at its highest aspect.

Such leaders exhibit awareness, sensitivity, and other traits such as:

(i) *High emotional intelligence.* Their sensitivity allows them to feel people's emotions deeply and they take greater care in helping people get through their issues and problems. This creates a happier work environment for everybody to do their best. At present, those who are often applauded are leaders who are tough-minded and strong, and those who push people to extremes to get the best out of them. However, many studies have currently shown that a more effective leader is someone who gives comfort and emotional support to their followers. That kind of leadership helps people feel encouraged to keep doing their best – all because they feel valued and appreciated.

(ii) *Honesty and integrity.* People have to believe that their leader has integrity. Leaders with high EQ are generally more honest and authentic, and they garner more trust. As a result, this makes people more likely to listen and follow their direction.

(iii) *Inspirational.* Such leaders have the ability to touch people's hearts. Inspiring people involves knowing the words that hit the right tone and the right message. Feeling emotions and operating from the heart intensely give them an advantage in expressing themselves in a powerful way. That can really motivate and inspire those around them to work harder. People are quick to follow others who show their passion for their beliefs and values.

(2) The second level of the intellect is the activity level associated with passion, ambition, and energy, called Rajasic in Sanskrit. This relates to the logical, reasoning, dry critical aspect of the intellect. This is the domain of modern science and the part of the intellect that is worshipped by modern society. However, it is insensitive to nature and life due to the dominance of emotions such as greed, selfishness, and unbridled ambition (all displayed in ample measure in modern society) and does not have total purity of intent.

Neuroscience states that mental processes that we are not conscious of, drive our decision-making, and logical reasoning and is often no more than a way to justify emotional choices. Fewer leaders, however, realize how much their own emotional state influences a team's (or an organization's) attitude and productivity. Strong leaders must have robust and balanced thinking skills along with the qualities of empathy and love as mentioned earlier. These skills are critical prerequisites for high performance as they are needed to process information and then communicate clearly business plans and strategies. Leaders must know how to manage words and information.

Achieving good balance in thinking depends on four key attributes:

(i) *Logic.* Logical thinking keeps us organized, predictable, and successful, particularly when looking to fit and/or match a specified outcome. This type of thinking is important in standard work, lean manufacturing, and areas where repeatable systems are critical for quality or reliability.

(ii) *Creativity.* Creativity is important for innovative, inventiveness, and arriving at new and unique possibilities. While logic tends to build on what is known and proven, often "outside the box" creativity can produce more positive solutions than the first obvious logical choices.

(iii) *Attention to detail.* How does one balance awareness of all the details around him/her without getting buried in the fine details? Some jobs, or parts of a job, benefit from high attention to detail where others rely more on a big picture focus.

(iv) *Learning.* Finally, how avidly and consistently does an individual acquire new information and experiences to broaden and enrich his/her thinking resources?

A leader with critical thinking skills can understand the logical connections between ideas, identify the relevance and importance of arguments, detect inconsistencies or mistakes in reasoning, and make proper decisions.

There are leaders who are clearly intelligent and good at coming up with the right answer, but they make questionable decisions. Then there are leaders over the years who have had great people skills, could inspire those around them and are good at implementing solutions. Many leaders are incapable of thinking through the implications of a potential scenario and cannot properly evaluate options they are faced with, or detect a flaw in someone else's logic, and often make wrong decisions, displaying their lack of critical thinking skills. To be a good critical thinker, one has to be able to not only gather information but also assess the relevance of these options. How critical are they to the situation and which piece of information will have the most impact on the problem at hand. How probable is one consequence over another? Which assumptions can one rely upon and what are the ones he/she should question? All of these are important questions that help people refine their judgement and make thoughtful decisions.

(3) The lowest level of the intellect stems from dogmatism, rigidity, pessimism, ignorance, laziness, etc. (called Tamas in Sanskrit). This relates to the dogmatic, fixed intellect that holds on rigid fixed intellectual concepts such as communism, socialism, democracy, and other fixed rigid ideas. The following chart gives an overview of Buddhi.

Level	Guna (Attribute)	Relation to intellect
Higher	Sattva	Discriminating, humanitarian, feeling
Middle	Rajas	Logical, critical, reasoning, scientific
Lower	Tamas	Dogmatic, fixed, rigid concepts

How Does One Develop Discrimination?

Discrimination can only be developed by the constant use of the intellect. This means that the intellect has to be developed at three levels:

- At the level of conscious discrimination, which is feeling, caring, and sensitive thought.
- At the level of logical, critical, reasoning, scientific thought.
- At the level of the dogmatic, fixed, rigid concepts.

The intellect has to be used by observation, analysis, and judgement. The application of logical reasoning is based on direct perception and an objective enquiry as an impartial observer into unexplained events. This requires the subjugation of the emotional mind to the intellect along with a critical examination of the motives of one's actions. Emotions (energy in motion) can be used very effectively in a positive way for achieving results provided they have the intellect as a guide. For example, for a senior executive who has the responsibility to ensure that targets are achieved, rather than let the "fear of failure" which is a negative emotion, one can use the positive emotions of "trust and kindness" to achieve one's goals. This will translate into building a team, sharing the goal, coaching for skills and empowerment rather than hire and fire which will be what the first emotion will lead to.

A simple example is that which most modern people have experienced at least once or twice in their life – the confusion of the workplace with the home. On a professional level we are generally forced to behave in a certain manner, which is appropriate for our profession, be it window washing or management. However, humans often end up continuing to behave in the same manner at home with their spouse and children. This has been the cause of more than a few divorces. It is hard for the conditioned mind to change roles, and even harder to become aware of its own conditioning.

It is only through developing the higher side of Buddhi that mind conditioning can be observed. If the intellect is not developed slowly, then self-observation becomes difficult or impossible. Stronger demands on the conditioned mind make it harder for the intellect to function on its higher, discriminative level. One example of this could be a managerial position that has tremendous responsibilities. These responsibilities force the individual to increase the strength of the mind to survive and do well. Slowly the individual will lose the power of self-observation unless a conscious effort is made to develop it directly. This is why many CEO types are very difficult to be around on a personal level. It must be emphasized that it is important to develop the intellect not only in its rational, logical function but equally important (but is very often neglected) is the development of the feeling, discriminating fire of perception. This results in so much perversion in corporate life as can be seen with immoral/heartless action taken with a view of protecting bottom lines without regard to the effect it has on the lives of the people who work there. Another example is the disparity in the pay between CEOs and others.

Developing the Mind and Intellect

From our discussions earlier, it is now clear how the mind and the intellect can be strengthened.

(i) The emotional mind must be kept in check by making it subservient to the intellect. In scientific parlance the amygdala must be kept in check through meditation, whatever the form that it takes.
(ii) The three parts that constitute the intellect should be strengthened through

(a) Visualization exercises that negate the negative trait mentioned below and strengthen the positive trait.

Purity	Intelligence, flexibility, peace, intuition, clarity, happiness, self-love, compassion, understanding, creativity, caring, humanitarian.
Activity	Agitation, anger, jealousy, frustration, overbearing ego, aggression, overuse of stimulants (coffee, etc.), motivated, goal seeking, workaholic.
Inertia	Inflexibility, dullness, stupidity, violence, perversion, depression, unhappiness, lack of love, drug addiction, delusion, deception, dishonesty.

(b) Developing logic and reasoning skills and critical thinking ability along with the ability to express clearly.
(c) Spending time in self-introspection and self-observation to examine the roots of one's beliefs.

In modern society, we are mentally a mix of the three Gunas or attributes, namely Sattva (purity), Rajas (activity), and Tamas (dullness). Our culture demands a Rajasic mentality and often we become fixed in ideas or emotions that indicate Tamas. The ancient methodology is to increase Rajas to move the inert Tamas, hence the recommendation to do social service as a means to rise above dogmas and fixed ideas. A dull inert Tamasic mind cannot be changed directly – one has to use Rajas (dispersing action) to diminish the inertia of Tamas. At present, Pure Sattva is basically unheard of, as our culture does not support it. If someone claims to be completely Sattvic or pure, then most times it indicates a dominance of self-delusion.

It is also important to acknowledge that a dominance of Tamas does not mean that the person is violent or a pervert. It usually manifests as depression, lack of love, unhappiness, or just blindness to one's real state. These are the most common mental problems of our culture and they are all related to Tamas. Alternatively, high Rajas does not necessarily mean that the person is an egoist and overbearing. The modern type "A" person is classically Rajas. This type is the over-working type with the inability to stop "achieving" and that indicates very high Rajas.

One of the primary ways to develop the higher discriminative powers of the intellect is to promote purity in the mind. The predominance of Rajas (activity) gives one an analytical, logical, intellectual mind, but also one that is unfeeling and mechanical. Predominance of Tamas drives the Buddhi downwards into the emotional mind and sense pleasures, and the continual need for stimulation to activate the dullness of the mind.

Another key to develop the Buddhi is through the impressions we receive from our environment. If one is living in a violent neighbourhood, it tends to promote either fear or its opposite which is violence. By the same token, watching violent movies will increase one's own anger, frustration, and violence. The increase of violent crimes among the young in relation to the increase of media violence is an obvious example.

Hence, the selection of what we allow into our senses will affect our mind. A man looking at pornography will always be thinking of sex. A woman looking at clothing catalogues will be often thinking of buying new clothes. A child watching TV and seeing the new toys will want to have the latest toy.

Limiting or choosing what is received into the conditioned mind helps to promote the intellect because the downward movement is lessened. This is important for our children as well. They should be given structure and TV time that depicts violence and sex should be limited and controlled. This is not being moralistic but being practical as that is the way the human mind grows and evolves.

Another key impact is had by the food one takes. This also has an effect on the mind and so ultimately the intellect. Modern research shows that certain food additives change behaviour of both children and adults. What we take into our bodies on the sense impression level conditions the psychology and what we take into our mouth conditions the metabolism. Hence a diet based on pure foods is one of the ways that psychology of transformation uses to promote the higher aspects of Buddhi, the intelligent principle of discrimination and self-observation.

The other side of this is the expression of the impression received. If we intentionally hurt or harm others – emotionally or physically – it pulls the intellect down into the lower sensual mind. Hence, expression is as important as reception. If one is creative and brings new knowledge or beauty to the world, it is a way to develop the intellect. If the expression is destructive, damaging, and against knowledge and beauty, then it brings down the intellect into a negative state, hence the need to desist from frequent negative arguments.

Therefore, the practical thing that we can do in life to preserve our health mentally and physically is to limit the intake of impressions and food to pure, healthy material. How we express ourselves on both a personal and social level is equally important. Additionally, we can strive to promote the higher ideals of humanity in our consciousness. These are fundamental steps for reversing the downward movement of creation. They are important and provide the foundation, but they represent the beginning.

Logical Reasoning and Critical Reasoning

Research conducted in recent years by a variety of independent academics has shown that people need the following skills in a corporate context to do well:

- Good analysis and problem-solving skills
- Good judgement and decision-making
- Good overall job performance
- The ability to evaluate the quality of information presented
- Creativity
- Job knowledge
- The potential to move up within the organization.

Pearson has developed the following RED Model – Recognize Assumptions, Evaluate Arguments, Draw Conclusions – as a way to view and apply critical thinking principles when faced with a decision:

- *Recognize Assumptions*. This is the ability to separate fact from opinion. It is deceptively easy to listen to a comment or presentation and assume that the information presented is true even though no evidence was given to back it up. Noticing and questioning assumptions helps to reveal information gaps or unfounded logic. Taking it a step further, when we examine assumptions through the eyes of different people (e.g. the viewpoint of different stakeholders), the end result is a richer perspective on a topic.

- *Evaluate Arguments.* It is difficult to suspend judgement and systematically walk through various arguments and information with the impartiality of a Sherlock Holmes. The art of evaluating arguments entails analysing information objectively and accurately, questioning the quality of supporting evidence, and understanding how emotion influences the situation. Common barriers include confirmation bias, which is the tendency to seek out and agree with information that is consistent with one's own point of view or allow emotions to get in the way of objective evaluation. People may quickly come to a conclusion simply to avoid conflict. Being able to remain objective and sort through the validity of different positions helps people draw more accurate conclusions.
- *Draw Conclusions.* People who possess this skill are able to bring diverse information together to arrive at conclusions that logically follow from the available evidence, and they do not inappropriately generalize beyond the evidence. Furthermore, they will change their position when the evidence warrants doing so. They are often characterized as having "good judgement" because they typically arrive at a quality decision.

A discriminating mind is very much required for enabling logical and critical thinking.

DISPASSION (THE SECOND D)

Dispassion refers to the absence of or control of negative emotions such as desire, passion, and addiction. So absence of or freedom from addiction or total slavery to sense pleasures is called dispassion. Discrimination on the kinds of sensory pleasures and the addiction to it and indulgence in moderation is the key for a healthy mind. A person who is addicted to sense pleasures will end up spending all one's energy in the indulgence of such pleasures. This results in the dissipation of one's mind and energy and the consequent inability to focus on achieving what one has set out to do. Being dispassionate does not require a lack of passion; it requires self-awareness and self-control. It requires the use of the intellect to evaluate situations based on objectivity and without personal bias and prejudices or at least with the recognition of the same.

In a sense it is also a measure of detachment with a focus on the action at hand without undue concern on the results, a lesson so forcefully taught in the *Bhagavad Gita.* Addiction to results is also a form of addiction that limits forceful action.

The American psychologist and placer of self-actualization at the top of the pyramid, Abraham Maslow, said "Dispassionate objectivity is itself a passion, for the real and for the truth." We should be dispassionate with a passion. Even in pursuing our passions, we should temper it with a degree of dispassion. To be dispassionate is not to be influenced by strong emotion, and thus to be unbiased, impartial, rational, and cool. Dispassionate people are able to coolly and rationally assess situations, free from bias and prejudices, make sense of data, and arrive at sensible decisions.

To quote Pete Caroll, one of the legendary American football coaches and who is the Head Coach and Executive Vice President of the Seattle Seahawks of the National Football League (NFL)

> "If you can get your mind right, you can be at your best. So, what does it take to get your mind right? It all comes down to focus."

Focus requires a quiet mind. Fear and distractions are the two biggest culprits that rob us of the ability to quiet our minds and neither can coexist with focus. They quickly become discursive thoughts that pull one away from being his/her best. That is why we always strive to play or work in the absence of fear and distractions.

The Freedom of Focus

Focus flows from confidence and trust. When one has confidence in his/her preparation and abilities and trust in him/herself and his/her teammates (on the field or in the office), then he or she is freed up to be able to focus on what is in front of him/her in the moment. And when one is truly focusing, there is nothing to worry about and nothing holds him/her back from being his/her best. Confidence comes from the process of preparation; through practice and effective training, one gains awareness and assurance of his/her ability. Confidence is connected to knowing the truth – the truth about oneself and one's abilities. And at the foundation of confidence, one has got to know who he/she is and what his/her philosophy is, so that he/she can operate from truth. Confidence lays the groundwork for one to be able to trust him/herself and the people around him/her, because he/she has seen the preparation and knows that he/she and his/her teammates are ready to make the most of the opportunity in front of him/her.

Focus Training

Confidence and trust get one's mind to the optimal place to achieve focus. When confidence and trust are working hand-in-hand, focus flourishes. One will have a knowing beyond all knowing that he/she is going to be his/her best. Training one's ability to focus allows him/her to work, play, and perform like he/she is capable. That is all we can ask for! If we can simply perform like we are capable, then we are really hard to beat. So when one is focused, he/she is at his/her best. And there is nothing better than that.

This is a focus on the action stemming from knowing what one wants to achieve, preparation, and hard work. Results will follow deliberate action. This what the Bhagavad Gita means when it says focus on the action and not the results.

There is no doubt that passion is important, both as a source of energy in our lives individually and within group efforts, however detached attachment is the key to success.

In a management context, this will translate to scenarios described as follows.

Gathering Facts of the Situation

While collecting data for decision-making, bias needs to be eliminated. Passion, prejudice, and bias are usually the reasons for wrong data collected and interpretation of data. A dispassionate mind would go a long way to objectively look at the data not from a view of the results but from a view of interpreting the data to take corrective action. For a good market researcher or an analyst, dispassion is a key requirement.

Evaluating Investment Decisions

In problem solving, better decisions are made when we seek the advice and counsel of others, use long-term thinking, and look at options on their merits in terms of how they address root causes, rather than how we feel about a particular solution. In other words, the use of the intellect rather than the emotional mind is called for. The approach of Warren Buffet in consistent decision-making and his good track record are built on this principle rather than on any emotions.

Self-reflection and Self-analysis

Self-reflection and self-analysis is the key to personal growth both as a person and as a leader. Looking back on one's mistakes either on a day-to-day basis or as part of a project review can arouse strong emotions. It is fine to have these emotions, but the skilled leader or change agent brings a dispassionate approach to stating the facts and leading the discussion around lessons learnt and the way forward.

Listening to Customers

Listening to customers is probably the greatest tool of successful businesses. This calls for an approach which is not only enthusiasm and emotions led, but also which relies on listening to the voice of the customer dispassionately.

To a large extent, developing the intellect helps in developing dispassion.

DISCIPLINE (THE THIRD D)

The third inner strength is discipline. The inner strengths that are required in life as well as in the corporate world or indeed in any activity are

- Mind control
- Sense control or control of sensory faculties
- Withdrawal or quietude
- Endurance, patience, forbearance, etc.
- Faith or trust
- Concentration and focusing power.

While we talk of mind control and concentration, it is far more effective if we develop our strengths in all of the above. They support and complement each other.

It all boils down to self-discipline. Specifically, it is important that one is self-disciplined with one's daily choices.

Here is a story that articulates the importance of self-discipline and self-awareness very well. This is a story that was recounted by an American, Russel Herman Conwell who later became a clergyman, and was initially a lawyer for 15 years. He recounted this over 6,500 times. He is best remembered as the founder and first president of Temple University in Philadelphia, and for his inspirational lecture, "Acres of Diamonds." The central idea of this story is that one need not look elsewhere for opportunity, achievement, or fortune; the resources to achieve all good things are present in one's own community. This theme is developed by an introductory anecdote, credited by Conwell to an Arab guide, about a man who wanted to find diamonds so badly that he sold his property and went off in futile search for them. The new owner of his home discovered that a rich diamond mine was located right there on the property. The story goes as follows: A farmer in Africa got excited about diamonds and sold his farm and went all over Africa in search of diamonds. He never found any and finally broke and desperate, committed suicide. Meanwhile the new owner of his farm picked up an unusually looking rock and put it on his mantle. A visitor told him that the funny looking rock was the biggest diamond in the world. The owner told the visitor that the farm was filled with such rocks. This became the Kimberly diamond mine which is the richest diamond mine the world has ever known. The original owner was sitting on acres of diamond. Each of us are sitting on our own diamond mines if we could only realize and develop our own strengths. He told the story to thousands and raised US$6 million for the Temple University which is a great institution in American education.

"If you want to achieve the things you want dare to dream and build the future yourself ... believe and hope it is going to happen. If you want to get the most from your acres of diamonds, then you need discipline and specifically self discipline. Also required is the willingness and ability to sacrifice what you want now for what you want more later on."

Mind Control

Mind control is equanimity, peace, poise, or tranquillity of the mind, which basically means that the mind is free from stress and strain. At present, stress is a very big problem that everybody faces. A stressed, tensed, or anxious mind becomes a burden, and for a person who does not have peace of mind, the mind itself becomes a burden. At present, among youngsters and also people in the corporate world, stress has become a way of life and this in turn leads to addictions of various sorts.

When the mind enjoys peace and freedom from stress, the mind is a light mind which is an effective instrument for accomplishing our goals. The difference between other animals and a human being is that we alone are endowed with a superior mind which is capable of accomplishing any type of goal, be it material or spiritual.

So, peace of mind is required first for our very survival itself and is also an essential prerequisite for maintaining physical health. A person who has stress consistently for a long time is bound to have varieties of physical problems. Furthermore, even our intelligence can be utilized effectively only when the mind is calm. When the mind is disturbed, however educated one may be, however rational one may be, all the knowledge that we have, cannot be effectively accessed and utilized. This is similar to a virus-infected computer where the information stored becomes inaccessible. Similarly, all our knowledge, all our studies, all our IQ, etc. will be useless when the mind is disturbed. And that is why management gurus have been harping on EQ to make IQ more effective. A balanced mind is important to use our knowledge effectively. Thus, peace of mind is required for maintaining physical health, intellectual health, and spiritual journey.

So, the first discipline is stress management. We should learn to enjoy a poised mind. The best way to control mind wavering as has been explained elsewhere in this book is initially through breath control and then meditation.

Sense Control

Sense control is the mastery or control of the sense organs. As indicated earlier, the external sense organs are five (eyes, ears, nose, skin, and tongue) and the mind is the internal sense organ. Control or management of the sense organs does not mean suppression, rather it should be an intelligent direction or intelligent channelizing of the sense organs. Any form of suppression is dangerous because it has the potential to explode later. We should restrain the sense organs and allow sensory energy to go only after we exercise our intellect. It is similar to building a dam across a river. Water that is otherwise wasted is stored and channelled for effective use when required. Similarly, sensory control is not allowing the sensory energy to go wherever it wants but channelizing its direction.

Control of sense organs is extremely important because our mental condition is dependent on our sense organs. The sense organs are the doors for the external world to enter our mind. They decide which part of the world and which sound must enter us, which form must enter us, which smell must enter us and if these organs are not properly managed, there is a free flow of sensory perception into our mind which leads to conflicts and disturbances. We therefore need to have proper checks and control and reduce or eliminate those sensory inputs that can cause mental turbulence. This is very important for mental health and is directly related to mind control or mindfulness.

Withdrawal or Quietude

Withdrawal or quietude is required to maintain and preserve the peace of mind, which has been acquired through mind control. This means preventing any disturbance. So, the difference between mind control and quietude is that the former refers to calming the disturbed mind and latter refers to maintaining that calmness. So, the remedy for disturbance is mind control and the prevention of disturbance or maintenance of the peace of mind is quietude. One is a treatment and the other is a prevention.

Endurance or Forbearance

> The American Civil War began in April 1961. No one at that time could imagine that this would continue for another 4 years. The casualty counts started growing. Lincoln's capacity to think, to see the big picture, to consult lots and lots of people kept pace. One of the really important aspects that Lincoln exhibited in the moments of crisis leadership was forbearance or emotional discipline. The most striking incident is the one that happened right around the Battle of Gettysburg, which occurred in July 1863 in Pennsylvania town. This was a crucial battle. Robert E. Lee, who led the Army of Northern Virginia, the biggest Confederate fighting force, had invaded the north. On the opposing side, in a small town in Pennsylvania, was George Meade, who was the commander of the largest Northern fighting force, the Army of the Potomac. The two armies fought it out over 2½ days. Lee lost, turned his army around, and immediately began moving his men and a wagon train of wounded confederates that was 17 miles long, back south. Meade made a critical decision that afternoon and confirmed it the next day that he was not going to pursue Lee. He decided that his soldiers were too exhausted to give hot pursuit. When Lincoln got this news from Meade, he was absolutely enraged. His line of thinking was that if Meade could pursue and squash Lee's army, the war would effectively be over. A furious Lincoln wrote a very strongly worded letter in the heat of the moment – something that we all tend to do when our emotions hold sway. Lincoln's letter talked of such things as, "Your decision not to pursue General Lee's army has extended the war immeasurably. Thousands more will die. You have made a huge mistake and I am immeasurably distressed and disappointed." And then he folded the letter up and put it in an envelope and he wrote on the envelope: "To George Meade, from Abraham Lincoln, July 5th, 1863. Never signed, never sent." And he put it in a cubbyhole in his desk, where it was found after he died. And that was a measure of Lincoln's self-discipline. Lincoln used that power to discipline himself to think ahead, to just take a breath, and to let his emotions cool over and over again, – a very important lesson in self-discipline.

Endurance is considered to be a very important and useful discipline, especially in dealing with day-to-day affairs. This is based on the idea that we all face painful experiences in life from time to time. Some of them are in the form of physical pain and some of them are in the form of mental anguish. The unfortunate fact is that when we go through pain, be it physical or mental, it invariably results in the mind becoming disturbed. As discussed earlier, a disturbed mind is operating at very low productivity. Hence, every human being has to find a method of handling pain.

What is normally done when faced with challenges is to find an external solution or a remedy for the pain by bringing about the appropriate changes in the conditions. Sometimes this is effective, but often the solution is unworkable either because it is physically difficult or financially very expensive. The other method is to go on tolerating the pain because there is no remedy, the remedy is very expensive, or we know that the remedy would lead to some other pain. Whatever be the reason, we go on experiencing the pain because of which pressure mounts up in our mind and body. A time comes when we are no longer able to handle the pain. And then the only solution we find is to convert the pain into anger or otherwise react emotionally. In an organizational context, there are often situations when it is not possible to let off steam because of the hierarchy or process-related reasons. Hence this is unexpressed and suppressed and this results, after a period of time, in an implosion, resulting in a lot of psychological damage.

However, another better method, not usually adopted or thought about, is to use our inbuilt capacity to tolerate and/or withstand pain. This is called endurance or tolerance. Everybody possesses the capacity for tolerance with differing threshold levels. While an external situation remains the same, reactions are different from different individuals primarily because of the difference in threshold levels of tolerance.

When the pain is within the threshold limits or tolerance levels, we do not experience it as pain at all. Therefore, the trick is to find out a method by which the threshold levels are gradually increased by appropriate understanding and practices. If we can thus increase the threshold, the mind deals with it differently. Endurance means increasing the level of tolerance, patience, immunity, or resistance power, both physically and mentally. Similar to a healthy body that is immune to diseases that are around, a healthy mind also has a high resistance or tolerance power. At the physical level it is called endurance, and at the mental level it is called forbearance or patience.

Faith or Trust

Whenever we undergo a medical treatment, it is very important that we have faith in the doctor and also the course of treatment that he prescribes. Even modern medical system advocates this principle. If the patient does not have faith in the doctor, even the best of the medicines will have reduced efficacy. Researchers have found that the reverse is also true and that if the patient has full faith in the doctor, even a placebo will work wonders.

Here is a lovely story on self-belief. One day Thomas Edison came home and gave a paper to his mother. He told his mother that his teacher gave this paper to him and said, "Give this to your mother." His mother opened it and read the paper. After reading the paper, her eyes filled with tears. Thomas asked his mother about what was written in the paper. She read the whole letter in loud voice to her son, "Your son is a genius. This school it too small for him and we don't have enough resources and good teachers to train him. Please teach him yourself." After many years, Edison's mother died and he had become one of the greatest inventors. One day while Thomas was looking into old family things he came across a folded paper in the corner of his desk drawer. He took it and opened it. He read the paper, "Your son is mentally ill and we won't let him come to school anymore." It was the same paper which was given to him by his teacher in school to give to his mother. After reading that Edison cried for hours and wrote in his dairy, "Thomas Alva Edison was an addled (mentally ill) child that, by a hero mother, became the genius of the century." The moral is that one should never ever give up. We need to be confident in ourselves and move ahead in life with a positive attitude, hard work, and self-belief.

In an organizational context, it is also very important to have faith or trust in someone either a leader or a colleague, someone with whom one can share his/her experiences and get an impartial opinion. At present, research has conclusively proved that "trust" is a key attribute that a leader should strive, among his/her people, to be effective.

INTENSE DESIRE AND DETERMINATION (THE FOURTH D)

It is an intense yearning, an intense desire, towards achieving the goal. For acquiring the goal, one should acquire both the knowledge and the skills for the same.

Striving is the key to success. Competition is not about getting the better of someone else. It is striving to be the best version of oneself.

In the words of Pete Carroll, "So constantly strive to be the best that's all we can hope for. Not focus to win the game but to play the best. Try to generate the top of your potential. It is usually mental. Try to find it and maintain it as much as you can."

In the words of the Indian tennis legend, Vijay Amritraj,

In the 1987 Argentina Davis cup match, when India was down and I was at the tail end of my career. I managed to win the 3rd set, just about. I was at the dressing room and the doc and physio was working on me and everyone saying you have done very well. Now stop it and go home as it could be injurious to your health. There is a point in every-one's life and career where there is a fork in the road, take a right and everything is comfortable and good and then there is a left turn which is practically filled with obstacles and challenges and bumps. It challenges your ability, your belief, and is a very high-risk proposition but this is where you are able to test yourself; to test your greatness and the potential to be great, just a 1% chance. But that is who I was and am and I took that choice. As Billie Jean King said 'pressure is a privilege and every challenge is an opportunity.' I won 6–2 fifth by the fifth set they already knew they were beaten. I played more than my ability but had self-belief on my side. It is not about winning or losing the match but the question is more about you as a person, your character and self-belief and that's the kind of thing that you want everyone to learn.

Purpose Aligned to Values

Pete Carroll spoke of his personal philosophy,

> Writing down your personal philosophy is a process that takes a lot of work, but everyone is capable of doing it. Living your philosophy is how we share who we are, what we stand for, and is the lens that guides our thoughts, words, and actions. Over the course of my career, I found myself getting fired a number of times. And the last time I was fired became the most significant one. Through the discomfort of being fired, which I thought was one of the worst times of my life, came some of the most important lessons that I've learned. Personally, I hate to learn the hard way, but in this case, it was one the most beneficial transitions that I was able to make, and it set me on course to where I am today. Sometimes, life looks so hard, and it feels so stressful, but this is an example of where perseverance can lead us to our best work. During that experience of getting fired, I went through the rigorous process of self-discovery. I realized that if I was going to get my act together, I better figure out what I'm all about. My philosophy guided my actions, as well as the actions of the team. We would compete to come back from this. It showed up in the language, with the way we stood up, dealt with it, and also with how we would use our approach moving forward. I don't think that there's anything more valuable than knowing who you are and what you stand for when you are facing challenges. It gives you the best opportunity to be resilient, to respond, to jump back into getting on course as soon as possible, and to return to being effective, as soon as possible. It also ensures that you do not react emotionally when threatened. We all have a way that is guided by our beliefs. We are all living by a philosophy, but you might not be able to articulate it. Doing the hard work – of writing down what's important to you and the words that make up who you are at your best – accelerates the self-discovery process.

In life, as in work, "purpose" holds the key. Goal clarity is key to achieving something. Therefore, it is very important that we take time off and define our goals – both for our life and for work related.

Both short- and long-term goals need to be defined clearly and prioritized. We should be clear about our immediate goal and our long-term goal. It should be thoughtfully decided, and once we have decided we should carry them in our mind all the time. Is the ultimate goal of our life merely earning money, securing food, clothing, and shelter, and producing some children? Is that the life's goal? If that is the goal, animals are better than humans because some of them do these tasks much more efficiently than humans. On the contrary, if our goals are something more exalted, we should take them very seriously and have a clear idea about our priorities. Writing them down and a constant reminder of these goals is key to achieving them.

Once these short- and long-term goals are fixed, we should always remember these two goals. This capacity to keep the goals in the mind all the time is called single pointedness. This decides our capacity to focus on the goals set by us and move towards achieving it. Success in any field requires concentration. We have seen all of these in detail earlier including why we should look at our goals everyday. From the scientific research that we have quoted earlier in this book, it is also clear that this purpose must also have deep meaning and be revisited everyday so that it becomes a part of the subconscious.

A sustainable goal that gives meaning to life is one that consists of

- Good or noble actions. A good action is defined as one in which the number of beneficiaries or the number of people who will benefit from the action is large. Higher the number of beneficiaries, superior is the action.
- Developing healthy virtues, healthy values like truthfulness, compassion, humility, consideration for others, etc.
- Developing a healthy attitude towards everything and everybody.
- Passion/skills sets/opportunity/meaning – the intersection of them.

Here is another fascinating story of a person with 11 Guinness World Records and a list of never before seen death-defying feats. Nik Wallenda has performed live in every state in the USA and all over the world from crossing the Grand Canyon and Niagara Falls to walking blindfolded between two towers in Chicago. Nik personified the Wallenda Family legacy of "Never Giving Up." On 4 March 2020, Nik completed his greatest accomplishment to date, walking over the lava lake of the active Masaya Volcano. Earlier, he had successfully completed the high-wire walk in San Juan that took his grandfather's life – a 135-foot-long high-wire crossing between the two towers of the 10-storey Condado Plaza Hotel. Nik shares how his worst fear came true when five family members fell while doing a stunt which gave rise to self-doubt "should I get back up on the wire?" He learnt from his family that they always fulfil their contracts. And so he did.

Some of his key takeaways from the high-risk job that he did are:

(i) It's my job as the leader to figure out who's shaky and be there for them.
(ii) Work to counter negativity with positivity and preparation.
(iii) One day you eat the chicken. The next day, you eat the feathers.
(iv) What you would call fear, I would call respect.
(v) The worst thing you can do for a wild animal is to show it fear. Show respect instead.
(vi) I never wear a harness unless my network partner makes me.
(vii) The preparation process for a big event is meticulous and intense.

  - It is all about building mental confidence.
  - Make training much harder than the event.
  - You cannot ever train enough.
  - If you think you should practise 5 times, do it 50 times.

(viii) Excellence is

- A passion about being good at what you do.
- Too many people are miserable at what they do. It is fear.
- Even if you hate your job, do it with excellence.
- You have to show up at work every single day.
- Be positive, force yourself to smile.

SUMMARY OF THE 4D PRACTICE

The 4D's		Impact on mind part	Technique	Area of brain impacted
Discrimination		Intellect (Buddhi), wisdom mind	Exercises for strengthening the intellect. Evaluation of situation and deliberate decisions not based on emotions alone. Developing will power (sample exercises will be described later)	Hippocampus – visual – spatial memory; establishing context; inhibiting amygdala and cortisol
Dispassion (detachment in action)		Intellect and restraint of the organs of knowledge	Meditation on emotions such as kindness, forgiveness, happiness, and trust	Inhibiting amygdala and cortisol
Discipline	Mind control	Emotional mind	Develop concentration and focus	Inhibiting amygdala and cortisol
	Sense control	Sense organs	Diet Body scan (yogic relaxation) Pranayama (control of energy through breath) Develop will power	PFC – executive functions; attention control Increased activation of left frontal regions, which lifts mood
	Quietude	Emotional mind, subconscious and sense organs	Meditation – watching the breath	Inhibiting amygdala and cortisol
	Forbearance	Mind	Develop will power	PFC – executive functions; attention control
	Faith	Mind	Faith meditation Visualization exercises	Inhibiting amygdala and cortisol
	Concentration	Emotional mind, memory (Chitta), and sense of ego	Prescribed sample exercises	PFC – executive functions; attention control Increased activation of left frontal regions, which lifts mood Increased gamma-range brainwaves – may be associated with integration, "coming to singleness," "unitary awareness"

(Continued)

The 4D's	Impact on mind part	Technique	Area of brain impacted
Desire (setting goals/ purpose to life)	Ego	Visualization Applying intellect Defining and aligning values to one's purpose Repeating and visualizing it everyday	PFC – executive functions; attention control
Beyond mindfulness meditation	All four parts of the brain	• Subtle physical exercises • Subtle yogic breathing • Releasing negative emotions • Awareness on energy centres • Yogic relaxation • Chakra (energy centre), meditation with mantras/ sounds • Light meditation	Positive impact on brain functions, hormones, and neurotransmitters. Leads to feeling of spontaneous well-being happiness. Conducive to the mental work of a knowledge worker.
Mindfulness in action	Part of daily life	Simple regular exercises	Way of life

This chapter brings all the individual parts into a comprehensive 4D practice which is what we had analysed as important attributes for life and leadership in Chapter 2. These chapters help in discovering one's purposes and aligning them with the values he/she holds dear while helping to define action plans. Some powerful and latest scientific findings on the pursuit of happiness are also explained.

Mindfulness and heartfulness will be discussed in the following chapter as it is practised widely, especially in the West, and is a very useful meditation tool.

13 Cultivating Mindfulness and Heartfulness

Mindfulness is a way of attending to the experience of the present moment in a way that is fully aware and without judgement or reactivity. It refers to a state of full attention on what is happening in the "now," i.e. the present moment. There is a wonderful book entitled *Power of Now* by the Buddhist Master Eckhart Tolle. His main message is to remind people that every minute one spends worrying about the future or regretting the past is a minute lost, because one has to really live in is the present, the now, which gives him/her actionable strategies to start living every minute as it occurs. The three major lessons that he expounded in his book are:

- Life is just a series of present moments.
- Pain is the result of resistance to the things one cannot change.
- One can free him/herself from pain by constantly observing his/her mind and not judging his/her thoughts.

In other words, to be a witness to one's thoughts as they arise. Easier said than done but that is the crux of mindfulness. Following the 4Ds that were outlined in the previous chapter, will to a large extent, help in being mindful and bringing the mind to the present moment.

Ellen J. Langer, Professor of Psychology at Harvard University, described mindfulness as "the process of drawing novel distinctions, or a heightened state of involvement and wakefulness," i.e. living each experience and each moment as new and in a conscious manner.

John Kabat-Zinn, one of the foremost authors on the subject, defines mindfulness as "the awareness that emerges through paying attention on purpose, in the present moment, and non-judgementally to the unfolding of experience moment by moment".

There are several other definitions but the common underlying thread is the "focus on the present moment" that one seeks to do consciously and non-judgementally.

Mindfulness is the capacity that we all share to be aware of what is going on in and around us in the present moment to cultivate a non-judgemental understanding of the situation. Actually, awareness is a better and more accurate expression. This fosters compassion and helps transform our health and well-being and makes us more alive to situations. It is not associated with religion though traditionally it has been practised by many religions and hence has a religious connotation. Mindfulness practice is the art of stopping, calming the mind, and looking deeply within to be aware of our thoughts. One cannot be mindful and be in the present moment, unless one's heart is at peace the mind will be floating in the past or in a fanciful future.This is not to stop our thoughts or force them away somewhere else but to be mindful of our thoughts. This helps us to develop insight into our thoughts, feelings and actions and understand the nature of what our thoughts and feelings are. This further leads to understanding and compassion. This fruit of mindfulness practice has the power to turn capitalism upside down. Currently capitalism is based on the worst that humans have to offer, greed. Mindful capitalism could support the well-being of people and the Earth, change the course of human existence, and stop the current course to planetary destruction, for which capitalism holds huge responsibility.

The Buddhists stress the importance of "mindfulness" – taking time out from the web of daily activities to relax and meditate. In fact, most mindfulness practices are borrowed from Buddhist practices. In the current corporate world, this has become a normal.

This is the story of Meher Pudumjee, the Chairperson of Thermax Ltd., who had to deal with the shock of losing father and brother in quick succession. She recounts how she was very angry with God and the world. Her mother Anu Agha was a huge pillar of strength. She attributed her recovery and that of her mother to Vipassana. This process helped her to come to terms with the loss and stop asking herself "Why me?" One should look around and see how many things he/she needs to be grateful for. "Vipassana gave me a sense of gratitude and a way to look at death." Her big learning was to try and cherish the relationships that matter to one when he/she is alive. This means living in the "now" and checking how one spends the time the present day.

Another compelling story is of Arthur Ashe who was the first black man to win the U.S. Open, Australian Open, and Wimbledon. During a heart surgery in 1983, he got infected by the blood that he received and contracted AIDS. From all over the world, he received letters from his fans, one of which conveyed: "Why does GOD have to select you for such a bad disease?"

To this, Arthur Ashe replied, "The world over 50 million children start playing tennis, 5 million learn to play tennis, 500,000 learn professional tennis, 50,000 come to the circuit, 5000 reach the grand slam, 50 reach Wimbledon, 4 to semi-final, 2 to the finals. When I was holding a cup I never asked GOD 'Why me?' And today in pain I should not be asking GOD 'Why me?' Happiness keeps you Sweet, Trials keeps you Strong, Sorrow keeps you Human, Failure keeps you Humble and Success keeps you Glowing, but only Faith and Attitude keeps you Going." Powerful words indeed.

Google offers an internal course called "search inside yourself" that has proved so popular that the company has created entry-level versions such as "neural self-hacking" and "managing your energy." The search giant has also built a labyrinth for walking meditation. eBay provides meditation rooms equipped with pillows and flowers. Twitter and Facebook are doing all they can to stay ahead in the mindfulness race. Evan Williams, one of Twitter's founders, has introduced regular meditation sessions in his new venture, the Obvious Corporation, a start-up incubator, and investment vehicle. The first reason is omni-connectivity. The constant pinging of electronic devices is driving many people to the end of their tether. Electronic devices do not only overload the senses but also invade leisure time. They feed on themselves: the more people tweet the more they are rewarded with followers and retweets. Mindfulness provides a good excuse to unplug and chill out – or "disconnect to connect," as mindfulness advocates put it. The second reason is the rat race. The single-minded pursuit of material success has produced an epidemic of corporate scandals and a widespread feeling of angst. Mindfulness emphasizes that there is more to success than material prosperity. The third reason is that "selling mindfulness has become a business in its own right." (*The Economist* – The Business of Mindfulness)

The benefits of mindfulness are well documented and researched and include better performance, better emotional intelligence, stress reduction (Mindfulness based Stress Reduction [MBSR] being probably the most used tool for mindfulness in the West), improved focus and productivity, and enhanced creativity at the individual level, social responsibility, and awareness at the organizational level.

Better emotional intelligence (EQ) in leaders at organizations helps in:

- More effective management styles, lesser conflicts
- Better manager–employee relationships
- Better teamwork
- Deliberate rather than rash decisions
- Conflicts handled more maturely and in a spirit of cooperation
- Creating a more positive work environment
- The impact of mindfulness on the corporate world and society.

While mindfulness as a practice has existed as part of traditions in the East for generations, its practice in the West and most particularly in business and the corporate world is more recent. For the last couple of decades, a lot of research has been going on to understand its impact in the workplace and has even begun to attract media attention from the likes of *The Economist*, *The Financial Times*, etc.

Mindfulness has begun to earn acceptance in the business world largely because of its positive results in improving stress, which has serious effects on performance and productivity. This is accentuated by the fact that the nature of the workplace is shifting from a production to a knowledge-based one. When a large number of knowledge workers in an organization adopt mindfulness practices, its impact and influence on the organization in a positive way has been observed. Hence organizations such as Google have made it as part of their regular programmes.

MINDFULNESS PRACTICES

There are several practices under the mindfulness umbrella. The most widespread mindfulness practice, called MBSR, was founded and developed in the field of healthcare and clinical psychology and has gradually spread to other fields such as education and executive training. It was designed by Jon Kabat-Zinn at University of Massachusetts in the 1970s. At present, programmes based on this method are used in a host of companies and organizations, in addition to its widespread application in clinics to treat and prevent stress and other psychological dysfunctions.

The MBSR training lasts 8 weeks and includes a variety of tools, all of which are borrowed from Buddhist practices:

- Seated meditation based on breathing: the most widely known is the practice of full attention
- Walking meditation
- Movements with awareness based on conscious movement techniques
- Body scans to improve knowledge of one's own body
- Breathing and relaxation techniques.

The effects of this method have been assessed in many studies, which document its positive effects on the brain, feelings of well-being, and emotional management extensively. In addition to MBSR, Davidson's (from University of Wisconsin–Madison) studies have also revealed relationship between different techniques and tools used and their effect on the brain and ultimately on one's emotional profile.

The techniques proposed by Davidson are similar to the ones used in MBSR, although he added compassion meditation that consists of consciously developing compassionate thoughts about oneself and one's environment.

There are many variations in this technique but essentially all mindfulness programmes have varying degrees of body scans, yoga, seated and walking meditation, and most importantly "attention" or "awareness" to thoughts and feelings in the present moment. Most of these techniques are from Buddhist and Eastern traditions including Indian traditions. It is currently universally acknowledged that most Buddhist traditions have its roots in Indian Tantric, Vedantic, and Agamic traditions prevalent in India where Buddhism was founded and evolved. However, at the root of such practices there are a number of other sub-practices that make mindfulness complete and effective and it is these thoughts and practices that have been elaborated in this book. The body of research and enquiry that has been done on mindfulness has shown its positive impact on the brain, as also its effectiveness on parameters such as health, stress reduction, emotion management, and so on. The author's hypothesis is that with the addition of some of the supplementary practices, the effectiveness of mindfulness will be both enhanced and long lasting and effective. It will also probably make the practice of mindfulness easier and more consistent. It would also be useful to understand the way Eastern Spirituality looks at consciousness and the human body, not so much from a current scientific perspective as we know science today but through contemplation, meditation, and insights.

One of the very effective ways in concentration and meditation is the use of mantras (sounds) and yantras (diagrams or symbols). Mantra sounds (root of "manas" meaning mind and "trayate" meaning direction) and yantra symbols are necessary tools of meditation and they have the ability to penetrate into the depths of the subconscious and unconscious mind where all past memories are stored. Concentration on these images and sounds alter our brain waves.

"From previous evidence of effective human biological response using various sounds and sonic vibration frequencies, certain sounds have been found to have a direct effect upon physiological systems (i.e. pulse rate, respiration, GSR, EMG pupillary dilation, EEG, EKG, body temperature, and others)" – Dr. Jeffrey Thompson, Founder/Director of the Centre for Neuroacoustic Research in Carlsbad, California. Centre for Neuroacoustic Research is a research centre, which is actualizing its vision of "Healing the Body*Heart*Mind and Spirit through the Scientific Application of Sound. Dr. Thomson's research has shown physical and psychological responses using electronically disguised nature sounds, including ocean, wave, water, wind, animal, human, organic, dolphin, etc., processed electronically in different octaves, speeded up and slowed down, processed through different filters, and embedded with specific frequencies for resonating brain waves into target states for opening the subconscious mind. Studies carried out in a variety of centres across the United States have seen positive physiological responses to the application of sound frequencies and music. One aspect of the current experimental projects which has received encouraging response is in the realm of "primordial sounds." These sounds consist of deeply recognizable sounds to the subconscious mind, i.e. nature sounds and physical organism sounds. It has been further found that these sounds have profound impact when they are disguised in such a way that the conscious mind does not recognize them. This then activates a mechanism similar to the subconscious programming response in which spoken phrases are speeded up or slowed down to unrecognizable values, yet the subconscious mind seems to easily hear the message and produce significant results in altered behaviour. By exposing test subjects to sound environments of disguised "primordial sounds," a state of subconscious "openness" seems to occur in which a heightened suggestibility of the mind occurs. In some cases, it appears that even neurohormone and autonomic body processes respond to specific sound frequency patterns. This opens up possibilities for this level of communication with higher brain function and has implications for the fields of psychology, learning, and healing.

Since ancient times, Indian healing systems and meditations have been using sound to enhance altered states of consciousness. The temple traditions and many meditation practices are all based on sound either in its audible or subtle form. In Indian yogic thought, sound has four divisions: *Para* that finds manifestation only in prana or energy and is extremely subtle; *Pasyanti* that finds manifestation in the mind as thought waves; *Madhyama* that finds manifestation in the Indriyas or sense organs; and *Vaikhari* that finds manifestation in articulate expression or as audible sound. Mantra is normally at these four levels though we are consciously aware of only the audible loudly chanted mantra and the silent chant in the mind. Sound in the subtle form is played within the mind to alter states of consciousness or access the sub/superconsciousness. Methods for delving deeper into the mysteries of the power of human consciousness to change our lives and control inner and outer forces of nature have been employed for thousands of years. China used meditation gongs; in Tibet, metal "singing" bowls, bells, cymbals, and chanting; in India, tamboura drums and a whole wealth of musical traditions based on the "tonic" note; and these and others were used in numerous other cultures across the world.

In fact, one does not need any advanced tools to hear the primal sound of "OM" which is a natural and continuous sound that can be heard all around within and outside when the mind is still and there are no external sounds that mask it. The ability to hear this sound is also a sign of the stillness of the mind.

In a pilot study entitled *EEG Spectral Analysis on OM Mantra Meditation*, the authors Harne, Bhavna P., Department of Electronics, S.S.G.M. College of Engineering, Maharashtra, India and Hiwale, A.S. Shegaon, Department of Electronics, MIT College of Engineering, Pune, India investigated the temporal dynamics of oscillatory changes after OM mantra meditation. Twenty-three naive meditators were asked to perform loud OM chanting for 30 minutes and the EEG was subsequently recorded with closed eyes before and after it. To obtain new insights into the nature of the EEG after OM chanting, EEG signals were analysed using spectral domain analysis. Statistical analysis was performed using repeated measures of analysis of variance. It did not reveal any specific band involvement into OM mantra meditation but significant increase in theta power was found after meditation when averaged across all brain regions. This is the main effect of OM mantra meditation. However, the theta power showed higher theta amplitude after the meditation at all regions in comparison with the earlier condition of meditation. Finding was similar to other studies, documenting a reduction in cortical arousal during the state of relaxation. The study argues for the potential role of loud "OM" chanting in offering relaxation.

Hence use of mantras, sounds that may or may not have any meaning but are used in meditation, helps to alter brain waves and hence consciousness. An altered consciousness changes our objective reality.

SIMPLE VISUALIZATION TECHNIQUES FOR A LEADER (HEARTFULNESS MEDITATION)

1. Forgiving oneself
2. Forgiving others
3. Gratitude. Being grateful to all who have made a contribution to your life – good or bad and who have allowed you to grow
4. Health and mental fitness
5. Courage and self-worth
6. Abundance. Creating abundance and prosperity and success
7. Self-awareness. Looking inward and watching your thoughts
8. Self-growth. Hardwiring peace, love, and contentment into your brain
9. Building strength and determination
10. Confidence. Releasing self-doubt and deepening your self-worth
11. Calmness and peace. Feeling balanced, cantered, and relaxed
12. Success.

KEY TAKEAWAY

Mindfulness and heartfulness are the themes discussed in this chapter as they are widely practised especially in the West and are very useful meditation tools. One cannot be mindful and in the present if one's heart is heavy and weighed down. The heart that refers to the core of one's being needs to be empty and at peace. No meditation is as effective as the one that brings in our positive emotions into play (also described as heartfulness meditation) and therefore this chapter discussed about visualization techniques that help to develop qualities of the heart such as compassion, gratitude, kindness, empathy, love, and so on. The following chapter provides a summary of the entire book and its potential impact on a person who follows some of these practices and its implications for leadership.

14 Implications for Leadership

Covid-19 is both a global health crisis and an international economic threat. The worldwide lockdown that still continues to some degree across businesses and industries poses a number of challenges for both employees and employers. Work from home (WFH), mass lay-offs, emergency workers, increased power to the bureaucracy, etc. have changed the way we work and live. Organizationally, the economic shutdowns have forced change in the way they treat workers, build new systems and processes to measure productivity for WFH workers, handle increased issues arising from loneliness and stress of their workers, etc. While Covid-19 abruptly upended normal work routines, it also caused an acceleration of trends that were already underway, involving the migration of work to online or virtual environments.

A Gartner (2020) survey of 229 Human Resources (HR) departments showed that approximately one-half of the companies had more than 80% of their employees WFH during early stages of the Covid-19 pandemic and estimated substantial long-term increase in remote work after the pandemic. The need for millions of workers to WFH in response to Covid-19 has accelerated recent remote work trends facilitated by the rise of connectivity and communication technologies.

The challenges that gig workers are known to face will sound familiar to those required to WFH since they include getting and staying organized; managing the heightened emotions associated with such work; figuring out and maintaining an identity so that those emotions do not disrupt the productivity upon which their survival depends; coping with loneliness while also seeking out and maintaining functional relationships that support the work; and establishing some semblance of a long-term career (Ashford *et al.*, 2018). While it would not have been anticipated prior to the pandemic, future research into understanding participation and participants in the gig economy – starting with the assumption of economic precarity as a fact of life (Petriglieri *et al.*, 2019) – now appears likely to offer relevance for understanding (mandatory) WFH.

As per Deliotte 2020 report, there are five fundamental qualities of resilient leadership which distinguish successful CEOs as they guide their enterprises through the Covid-19 crisis:

1. Design from the heart and the head. Resilient leaders are genuinely, sincerely empathetic. Resilience mixed with decisiveness and firmness where warranted are the hallmarks of a true leader.
2. Put the mission first. Resilient leaders are skilled at triage and are able to stabilize their organizations to meet the crisis at hand while finding opportunities amid difficult constraints.
3. Aim for speed over elegance. Resilient leaders take decisive action – with courage – based on imperfect information, knowing that expediency is essential.
4. Own the narrative. Resilient leaders seize the narrative at the outset, being transparent about current realities – including what they do not know – while also painting a compelling picture of the future that inspires others to persevere.

5. Embrace the long view. Resilient leaders stay focused on the horizon, anticipating the new business models that are likely to emerge and sparking the innovations that will define tomorrow.

All of the above call for resilience from both leaders and also knowledge workers. Leaders will need to imbibe and develop qualities of empathy, leading from the heart, communicating better and constantly with a sharp focus, dealing with failures and setbacks, and most importantly generating trust in their followers. Knowledge workers also need to develop their emotional quotient as we have seen in an earlier Chapter 3.

In short, leaders are faced with challenges both organizational and personal. Here is some crystal ball gazing:

(i) Covid-19 is, in the view of many people, a view that I subscribe to, only the beginning of a series of difficult issues that we need to face due to our excessive use of the dry intellect with no empathy and concern for other living beings and the environment. This is reflected in our actions whether it be genetic engineering, our complete lack of concern for other living beings whom we use for our excessive luxury, our food habits, or the destruction of the environment in the name of economic progress. While there is some lip service to environmental concerns in board rooms and multilateral organizations, this is too little late. We will increasingly see nature's reaction whether it be natural disasters such as earthquakes, floods, epidemics, or other disasters. Whether Covid-19 is man-made or otherwise, it reflects on our selfish actions where we refuse for the most part to live in harmony with nature.

(ii) Added to this is the increasing bipolar world which is either US centric (a declining world power) or China centric (an aspiring world power). This will reflect in actions where there could be a new world norm aligned to either of these two blocs that excludes or limits the other. This will obviously have an economic impact with resultant limitations on trade, a fight for resources, movement of labour, etc. We will possibly see a more restrictive world than what we have seen for the last several decades.

(iii) The rise of technology (in the top 5 companies worldwide in terms of valuation) touches upon every aspect of our life and has replaced traditional companies altogether in many areas, for example, Uber in taxi hailing, Paytm in payment mechanisms, and/or amazon in logistics and delivery among other areas.

(iv) The rise of uncertainty and kind of employment. As mentioned earlier in this book, the rise of artificial intelligence (AI) and internet of things (IOT) will impact the kind and numbers of employment available with the necessity for people entering the labour force to be agile enough to re-skill themselves continuously as also to deal with uncertainty and stress.

(v) Small localized work/jobs will become more significant for a large number of people everywhere as the cost and ability to travel become restricted. Apart from the pandemic (to which there seems to be no solution in sight at this point), experts are warning of increased natural disasters such as earthquakes and flooding.

(vi) Without wanting to appear overly pessimistic, as the National Geographic says in its 2018 edition of *Book Talk*, what would happen if there was a polar shift. Experts are suggesting is a distinct possibility and which is likely to happen sometime soon. What would be its impact on technology and networks something on which we are currently so dependent. From the electrical grid that powers our computers to the satellites that let us watch TV, we are dependent on the Earth's magnetic field which is anchored by the North and South poles. The Earth's poles have reversed hundreds of times and experts say it is overdue. If it does, the consequences for life on Earth are potentially devastating. Daniel Baker, from University of Colorado, who is an expert in radiation from the sun and how that affects our planet, said there is no question in his mind that parts of the planet will become uninhabitable. It will also deeply impact and disrupt our electromagnetic system, the electric grid, and all the things we consider part of modern civilization.

Dealing with such uncertainties both current and possible, leaders and individuals need to be resilient themselves as also build teams and people who are resilient and who share the qualities of empathy, trust, and other soft qualities which have so far been pushed to the backburner in our efforts at being ultra-competitive. Building resilience from the inside out will be a key requirement going forward for both oneself and key members of the team and the employees at large. All these establish the need for individuals and organizations to focus at the individual level and ensure that every resource from the lowest worker to the CEO takes efforts at self-development. They also need to work at increasing and sharpening their own abilities and resilience both in terms of their skill levels for the job as also the inner strength to deal with change, stress and uncertainty.

The development of flexibility and a willingness to embrace change will make one a more valuable member of the organization he/she belongs to. To recapitulate, the other skills one needs to develop are:

- Building skills and continuous learning
- Adapting to change frequently requires the effective use of all of one's acquired skills. In some cases, adapting to change will call for the use of other skills as well – skills that one might not yet have mastered, or even begun to acquire!
- The ability to adapt is the key
- Embracing technological change and learning how to use it for one's own benefit
- Increasing one's speed of response. Greater opportunities come to organizations that can respond quickly
- The ability to live with ambiguity and uncertainty. Most people do not like ambiguity and uncertainty that are major sources of anxiety and also facts of life in this fast-changing world.

All these call for

- Continuous lifelong learning
- Strengthening the mind to deal with uncertainty
- Learning how to control one's emotions and deal with worry and stresses; in fact thrive on them.

The place to start is oneself, i.e. understanding and making oneself robust and strong physically, mentally, emotionally, intellectually, and spiritually.

ADVANTAGES OF INTEGRATING MEDITATION IN THE WORKPLACE

Although many of the benefits of meditation described earlier can and do affect individuals in all areas of their lives, including work, mindfulness' impact on job performance may be the outcome that gets the most attention and interest from managers and executives.

Meditation offers a means to deal with most situations difficult or otherwise in business, sports, or elsewhere and especially so in times of stress. A number of successful and well-known business practitioners have adopted and maintained the practice in their own work, crediting it for much of their success. Here are a few examples:

- Ray Dalio, founder of Bridgewater Associates, wrote in his book *Principles*:

  I came to meditation in my own life during a very stressful work period that then turned into a very stressful personal period. But it freed me from so much pain. It completely inverted my entire point of view on life. I've been meditating consistently … and I've seen an exponential impact. In terms of scale, the more you do the greater the reward. More than linear.

- Marc Benioff, co-founder and CEO of Salesforce.com, mentioned in an interview with the *San Francisco Chronicle*:

  I am very interested in keeping a clear head. So I enjoy meditation, which I've been doing for over a decade – probably to help relieve the stress I was going through when I was working at Oracle.

- Fred Wilson, a successful venture capitalist and co-founder of Union Square Ventures, wrote in his newsletter:

  I've been meditating for ten to fifteen minutes every day for the past two months … I am experiencing a number of benefits but the one I am most cognizant of is an increased ability to avoid distraction in a conversation or some other situation where I need to be focused. I've always been good at being focused, sometimes to a fault. But I also find my mind wandering in situations where I am losing interest and that's obviously very bad … Meditation is like repetitive exercise of the focus muscle in the brain. So if you are having trouble being present in situations you want to be but can't, I would strongly recommend trying meditation. It's helped me with this and I imagine it will help you too.

In their recent book *Altered Traits*, Daniel Goleman, a Harvard Psychologist, and Richard J. Davidson, a Neuroscientist at the University of Wisconsin, provide a scientific view of personal mindfulness benefits. They synthesize three proven benefits of mindfulness that, in combination, allow people to act more effectively in unpredictable environments:

- *Staying calm and open-minded.* Mindfulness practices, such as breathing meditation, are associated with decreased volumes of grey matter in the amygdala, the region of the brain that initiates a response to stress. This reduces the inclination to interpret an uncertain environment as a threat and thus react defensively. In this way, mindfulness improves mental agility, allowing attitudes to shift from "but we have always done it like that" to "let's see what happens if we try a new approach."
- *Cognitive ability.* Mindfulness improves short-term memory and the ability to perform complex cognitive tasks. It also frees people to think outside the box, which helps them cut through complexity. In the context of workplace performance, proven results include a higher quality of strategic decision-making and more effective collaboration.
- *Focus and clarity of thinking.* As Nobel laureate Herbert A. Simon observed, "a wealth of information creates a poverty of attention." This insight, first articulated in 1971, is more accurate currently than ever before. Maintaining a strong focus in this time of digital information overload, therefore, is essential. The regular practice of mindfulness routines can reduce mental wandering and distractibility. Mindfulness strengthens the awareness of both one's activities in the present moment and one's mental processes and behaviours (known as meta-awareness).

At the software company SAP, mindfulness has become a key ingredient of corporate life for employees and executives alike. More than 6,000 employees have taken 2-day mindfulness courses that focus on meditations complemented by the practice of self-mastery and compassion. In addition, internal mindfulness trainers offer guided meditations during working hours and a multi-week mindfulness challenge, including meditation "micro-practices," such as tuning out of a busy workday for a few minutes to focus on one's breathing.

Over the course of many years, Bosch, a multinational engineering company that focuses on automotive components and consumer goods, has increased its agility through a variety of initiatives. These include creating flexible organizational structures, introducing agile development methods, and experimenting with new business models and technologies. In order to promote the success of these initiatives, the company realized that it needed to fundamentally change its approach to leadership. According to Petra Martin, who is responsible for leadership development at Bosch Automotive Electronics, "Mindfulness is an essential lever to shift from a culture of control to a culture of trust. Communication has fundamentally changed since we introduced our mindfulness training to more than 1,000 leaders in the organization."

Aetna, a U.S. health insurer, has trained 13,000 employees on mindfulness practices, resulting in a reported reduction in stress levels of 28%. Annual productivity improvements, a secondary effect, are estimated at US$3,000 per employee. Aetna launched the mindfulness initiatives gradually, starting with brief meditations in executive-team meetings and then continuing with yoga and meditation classes for all employees. Mark Bertolini, Aetna's Chairman and CEO, said "We have demonstrated that mindfulness-based programs can reduce stress and improve people's health."

There are several ways that mindfulness has been shown to impact job performance, including:

- Gallant (2016) found that mindfulness meditation can improve executive functioning by improving inhibitory abilities.
- Mindfulness meditation in service industry workers improves job performance, even when controlling workers' level of engagement (Dane & Brummel, 2014).
- De Bruin *et al.* (2017) showed that meditation in the workplace can actually increase the number of contract hours worked by employees, a result that will certainly catch the attention of higher-ups.
- Office employees who participated in an 8-week mindfulness intervention experienced lower levels of work-related stress, greater job satisfaction, and, ultimately, enhanced job performance as rated by their employers (Shonin *et al.*, 2014).

Beyond job performance, mindfulness meditation has also been applied in the workplace for other benefits that can contribute to a healthy and productive work environment.

- Reduced work-related stress and psychological distress.
- Researchers such as Grégoire and Lachance (2015) found that call centre employees who took part in a brief mindfulness intervention reported decreased stress, anxiety, depression, fatigue, and negative affect, while also experiencing greater satisfaction at work.
- Similarly, employees from the Dow Chemical Company enjoyed *less stress* and increased resiliency and vigour after completing an online mindfulness intervention (Aikens *et al.*, 2014). Huang *et al.* (2015) also found that mindfulness reduces stress, fatigue, and psychological distress, especially for employees struggling with poor mental health.
- A study on mindfulness for public sector employees showed that this group was also able to benefit from the mental health effects of mindfulness. These employees reported less stress, reduced psychological distress, and improved social functioning and quality of life (Bartlett *et al.*, 2016).
- *Decreasing turnover and burnout.* Along with the decreases in stress, mindfulness can also lower the incidence of burnout and turnover at work.

- Researchers such as Taylor and Millear (2016) found that mindfulness helps employees construct a buffer between their work and becoming burned out. A study by Dane and Brummel (2014) also discovered an inverse relationship between mindfulness and turnover intention, meaning that employees who are higher in mindfulness are less likely to leave their jobs for any reason. The study referenced earlier by de Bruin and colleagues (2017) also uncovered the reduction in the risk of employees dropping out of work when mindfulness is encouraged in the workplace.
- Goodman and Schorling (2012) found that mindfulness-based stress reduction reduced work-related burnout and improved mental well-being among healthcare providers. A study by Australian psychologists added more support to this theory of mindfulness and burnout, finding a strong negative association between mindfulness and burnout (Di Benedetto & Swadling, 2014).
- Further research on mindfulness at work showed that mindfulness can act as a buffer for unsupportive work environments, enhancing well-being at work and contributing to lower levels of burnout for employees from a range of careers (Schultz *et al.*, 2015).

Here is a lovely story I once read with a strong message. In a school in India, two school-going friends rounded up three goats and painted the numbers 1, 2, and 4 on their sides. They then let the goats loose inside their school building that evening. The next morning, when the authorities entered the school, they saw goat droppings on the stairs and near the entrance and realized that some goats had entered the building. A search was immediately launched and very soon the three goats were found. But the authorities were worried, where was goat no. 3? They spent the rest of the day looking for goat no. 3 with frustration increasing as time went by. The school declared classes off for the students for the rest of the day with the teachers, attendants, and all others busy searching for the goat no. 3, which, of course, was never found as it was not there in the first place. Many of us, in spite of having a good life, are always feeling a "lack of fulfilment" and actually looking for the elusive, missing, non-existent goat no 3. If one lives in the present moment, the mind becomes meditative and life becomes a celebration.

The appendix provides a 1-hour routine to be followed at least 3–4 times a week and which can be made part of one's life. Guided meditation and some associated lecture videos on body scan and light meditation can be accessed at the author's YouTube channel.

Understanding the body better video is available at https://youtu.be/gS9PD94gd3k

The guided meditation is available on author's YouTube channel: https://youtu.be/iBkLr5Ncvyc

The guided meditation to body scan is available on author's YouTube channel: .

https://www.youtube.com/watch?v=yQ1NOzKF3ig&t=1100s (In this video, we take you through a body scan. The body scan is otherwise called yogic sleep or Yoga Nidra and it helps one deeply relax. This technique is widely used in the popular MBSR programme.)

Appendix 1 Start with the Physical

SUGGESTED PHYSICAL EXERCISES (20–25 MINUTES DAILY)

These are simple exercises but extremely effective and can be done on the go. They will ensure good health. It is suggested that they should not be overdone but should be done as per the capability and counts can be increased gradually. The following points are only indicative and they should be done with caution.

- Tap hard all over body including the head and the face with your fingers.
- With hands up and outstretched whirl around slowly (go around and round) on the balls of the feet. This is called the Sufi dance and it helps to balance the energy in the body (do it slowly; this may cause some giddiness, so do this with caution).
- Eyes exercise – Look up and down, sideways, up and down both sides at 45°, and finally rotate your eyes in circular motion. This will strengthen the eye muscles, providing you with good eyesight.
- Neck, hip, and knee rotation.
- Japanese bow – forward bend with hands outstretched – about 12 times up and down.
- Hands folded and bend back (backward bend) – 12 times down and up.
- Stand on toes and stretch.
- Sit as if on a horse and ride.
- Sit ups – clench fist when inhaling and open hands when exhaling.
- Rotate the shoulders and then place hands on shoulders and rotate.
- Bend front and inhale, and bend back and exhale.
- Bend forward and swing hands up and down.
- Sit on a chair and move hands in circular motion.
- Stand with feet, wide hands palm in front a little, and rotate on both sides.
- Bend sideways.
- March first with one leg and then another; one hand and leg up and neck back on one side and then another (5 minutes).
- Sit down in Vajrasana (kneel and then sit on the heels) and then up and down on knees.
- Stand on knees in Vajrasana and bend back with hands locked in front.
- Bend backward and lie in Vajrasana (slightly difficult and should not be attempted without supervision).
- Lie on back, bring leg close to body, so knees will be up. Twist leg from left to right chanting OM slowly; at the same time, turn head to the opposite direction (11 counts).
- Lie on front and lift leg – one leg at a time, then both legs simultaneously.
- Lie on front, lift head and legs, and touch (try at least).
- Lie on front side, lift head, shoulders, and back sideways, and spinal twist.
- Sit in Vajrasana and keep fists on Manipura on either side of stomach. Bend down and inhale as you go down.
- Sit in Vajrasana and then bend down similar to a baby pose.

Appendix 2 Breathe Easy and Live Life

SIMPLE AND EXTREMELY EFFECTIVE KRIYA PRANAYAMAS (TO BE DONE UNDER SUPERVISION AND NOT TO BE ATTEMPTED IF THERE IS AN EXISTING AILMENT)

- Deep breath in and out in a cross-legged sitting pose or sitting in a chair. Deep inhalation and deep exhalation without any gap between the inhalation and exhalation (5 minutes).
- Hands on lap, breath in stomach out and chest in with sudden force breathe out, and force shoulder back.
- Inhale deeply, bring in with hands brought in, and exhale and let go with force through mouth (as you breathe in visualize you are breathing in everything positive and good, and as you breathe out visualize that all the negative emotions such as fear, anger, and jealousy are going out).
- Kapalabathi Pranayama (passive inhalation and forceful exhalation).
- Ujjayi Pranayama. Neck breathing force wind in through epiglottis (neck region) and throw head back and then force wind down through throat with head down (two rounds).
- After neck breathing, from the earth take hands up and breathe in and exhale and take hands down; clean the aura in front of you with the earth energy.
- Alternate nostril breathing (two rounds fast and one round slow). Each round to be followed by one round of Bhastrika.
- Bhastrika is where you keep the hands near the shoulders as fists. Breath out, hands up palms open and facing outwards; breathe in and hands down to the shoulders as fists (50 times up and down is one round).
- Elemental breathing (slow inhalation through mouth visualize five bhootas coming in, exhale with force; hands out in front) to be alternated with the next exercise the kurma kriya.
- Kurma (Tortoise). Breathing (head up and breathe in through nose and head down breathe forcefully through mouth; hands at the Manipura chakra with left hand on top of the right hand) for three rounds. The back of the head should touch the top of the spine at the back and the chin should touch the top of the chest (throat) while neck down. Put hands left first and right over it on Manipura and bring chin to chest with inhalation through nose and then bend neck back with exhalation through mouth. Three rounds, and last round to be very slow.
- Surya Shakthi. Inhale through the right nostril, chin down retain breath as much as you can, then exhale through the left nostril (9/10 times). Bend forward and inhale deeply at varying speeds; increase speed and then reduce.

Appendix 3 Meditation: Light Up Your Life

A SIMPLE PERSONAL MEDITATION ROUTINE

- Sit comfortably. Slowly breathe deeply in and out. Inhale to the count of five and exhale to the count of five (or any equal number for in and out that feels comfortable to you) with no gap between the inhalation and exhalation. This deep slow breathing increases the pranic energies in your body. This is a simple pranayama exercise that will help to centre your Self and also align and energize the nadis with prana. I recommend that you breathe for at least 5/10 minutes in this way, but the longer you spend in deep breathing, the more effective it is.
- After about 5/10 minutes of this deep breathing, sit quietly and watch the mind. Do not attempt to control your thoughts or give them undue attention; just be aware. Watch them with dispassion. Become a silent observer of what is passing through your mind. Be aware, but do not participate by adding thoughts or sensations. Let your thoughts flow but watch them without judgement. Be mindful of what is transpiring in your inner universe. As you experience a thought, mentally say, "I am not this thought." In so far as you do not identify yourself with your stream of thoughts, you will begin to realize your Real Self. This process is not as easy as it seems for most of us. We have identified with our ways of thinking for a long time. But with ongoing practice, starting with a minute each day, it can be done. Ideally, after the first week of practice, add an additional minute each week until you can comfortably do it for 5 minutes at a time. You can experience major benefits in weeks or months. This is called the Neti technique. "Neti" means "I am not the thought."
- Then mentally chant "SO" as you breathe in and "Ham" as you breathe out. Watch the breath and stay in this state for about 10 minutes. The longer the better.
- Focus on the picture of the grace light reproduced below for a few minutes (2/3 minutes without blinking – in Yoga parlance this is called Tratak). Feel a ball of light coming from the centre of this picture into the middle of your eyes. Feel it!

In this meditation, the focus is only on the grace light. Now visualize grace as a vast white light pouring down from the top, coming down and into you through the top of your head. Visualize the vast grace light getting into every cell of the body. Feel the grace of the light in every part of you. Mentally chant the mantra "Arut Perum Jothi Arut Perum Jothi Thani Perum Karunai Arut Perum Jothi." Try and memorize this line, the literal meaning of which is "Let the most Desirable, Infinite Effulgent light, flow through me by the Grace and Mercy of the God of Light who is Omniscient, omnipotent, and omnipresent." If you find the Tamil verse difficult, then the English verse is fine. It is the feeling and attitude that is most important.

- As you mentally chant the mantra, visualize the white light entering you. Keep seeing the grace light go deeper and deeper into your cells.
- Now focus your attention at each chakra (2/3 minutes on each chakra – refer to Chapter 11 on chakras where the information on chakras has been given in detail) starting from the base chakra and continue upwards till you reach the crown chakra. If that appears complicated, just start with the body going up from the base of the spine to the top of the head – can do the chakras later in a guided meditation. Mentally chant the mantra and visualize the light spreading into you. (This is an extremely powerful mantra given by the great 19th-century Saint Ramalinga Vallalar who showed that it is possible to access one's light body.)
- Mentally chant/listen to the mantra until you finish the focusing and chanting till the crown chakra.
- As you do this process, you will feel that the energy, peace, and light (Jyothi) flowing through the crown into your heart and expand slowly through every cell, nerve, blood vessel, and consciousness. Let us go and enjoy the process without any expectation. Allow the Jyothi (the light) to do the process. The key is complete faith and surrender to the process.
- The attitude you must develop as you chant this mantra is one of faith and surrender and internalize this meaning and attitude:

  The Light is Supernal The Light is Eternal I Am the Light The Light is my Inner Radiance I Am the Radiant Light I Am the Radiance I Am Grace that fills the world.

- When you chant this mantra (mentally is the best way), you should always feel that you have already touched omniscience, omnipotence, and omnipresence. (Sound, light, and vibration constitute everything by which our own bodies are made up of and this meditation process touches upon all the three.) That is why it is called a Maha Mantra. It will bring about a total transformation/change in you and you can gradually feel the light entering inside you.
- You can also use this mantra and this Bhava (feeling) to remove any obstacle in your life, change relationships for the better, get anything physical/material/spiritual that you want as long as it is done with a Suddh Bhava (pure intentions) and you focus on your desire with concentration, faith, and patience. You can also use this process to heal yourself of diseases/illnesses. At the end of your meditation exercise, bring the object or the person in front of your mind's eye and wash it with the grace light as you chant the mantra. The key as I said is "pure intention." Any impure intention will backfire for sure.
- The whole process should take about 20–30 minutes. Even longer is fine.
- Finally, sit silently for a few minutes, and end the process with a feeling of gratitude to the masters.

Bibliography

BOOKS

Austin, J. 2009. *Selfless Insight.* MIT Press.
Begley, S. 2007. *Train Your Mind, Change Your Brain.* Ballantine.
Carter, C. 2010. *Raising Happiness.* Ballantine.
Hanson, R. (with Mendius, R.). 2009. *Buddha's Brain: The Practical Neuroscience of Happiness, Love, and Wisdom.* New Harbinger.
Johnson, S. 2005. *Mind Wide Open.* Scribner.
Keltner, D. 2009. *Born to Be Good.* Norton.
Kornfield, J. 2009. *The Wise Heart.* Bantam.
LeDoux, J. 2003. *Synaptic Self.* Penguin.
Linden, D. 2008. *The Accidental Mind.* Belknap.
Sapolsky, R. 2004. *Why Zebras Don't Get Ulcers.* Holt.
Siegel, D. 2007. *The Mindful Brain.* Norton.
Thompson, E. 2007. *Mind in Life.* Belknap.
Deep Work: Rules for Focused Success in a Distracted World by Cal Newport (Amazon).
Flow: The Psychology of Optimal Experience by Mihályi Csíkszenmihályi (Amazon).
Focus: The Hidden Driver of Excellence by Daniel Goleman (Amazon).
Good Business: Leadership, Flow, and the Making of Meaning by Mihály Csíkszentmihályi (Amazon).
Inner Game of Stress: Outsmart Life's Challenges and Fulfil Your Potential by Tim Gallwey (Amazon).
The Best Place to Work: The Art and Science of Creating an Extraordinary Workplace by Ron Friedman (Amazon).
The Culture Code: The Secrets of Highly Successful Groups by Dan Coyle (Amazon).
The Evolving Self: A Psychology for the Third Millennium by Mihály Csíkszentmihályi (Amazon).
The Rise of Superman: Decoding the Science of Ultimate Human Performance by Steven Kotler (Amazon).

SCIENTIFIC PAPERS

Atmanspacher, H. and Graben, P. 2007. Contextual emergence of mental states from neurodynamics. *Chaos & Complexity Letters*, **2**, 151–168.
Baumeister, R., Bratlavsky, E., Finkenauer, C., and Vohs, K. 2001. Bad is stronger than good. *Review of General Psychology*, **5**, 323–370.
Beauregard, M., Lévesque, J., and Bourgouin, P. 2001. Neural correlates of conscious self-regulation of emotion. *Journal of Neuroscience*, **21**(18), RC165.
Borders, A., Earleywine, M., and Jajodia, A. 2010. Could mindfulness decrease anger, hostility, and aggression by decreasing rumination? *Aggressive Behavior*, **36**, 28–44.
Brach, T. 2013. *True Refuge: Finding Peace and Freedom in Your Own Awakened Heart.* Bantam Books.
Braver, T. and Cohen, J. 2000. On the control of control: The role of dopamine in regulating prefrontal function and working memory. In *Control of Cognitive Processes: Attention and Performance XVIII.* Monsel, S. and Driver, J. (eds.). MIT Press.
Brefczynski-Lewis, J.A., Lutz, A., Schaefer, H.S., Levinson, D.B., and Davidson, R.J. 2003. Neural correlates of attentional expertise in long-term meditation practitioners. *Proceedings of the National Academy of Sciences of the U.S.A.*, **104**(27), 11483–11488.
Carter, O.L., Callistemon, C., Ungerer, Y., Liu, G.B., and Pettigrew, J.D. 2005. Meditation skills of Buddhist monks yield clues to brain's regulation of attention. *Current Biology*, **15**, 412–413.

Cherkin, D.C., Anderson, M.L., Sherman, K.J., *et al.* 2017. Two-year follow-up of a randomized clinical trial of mindfulness-based stress reduction vs cognitive behavioural therapy or usual care for chronic low back pain. *JAMA*, **317**(6), 642–644.

Craig, A.D. 2002. How do you feel? Interoception: The sense of the physiological condition of the body. *Nature Reviews Neuroscience* **3**, 655–666.

Craig, A.D. 2009. How do you feel now? The anterior insula and human awareness. *Nature Reviews Neuroscience,* **10**(1), 59–70.

Davidson, R.J. 2004. Well-being and affective style: Neural substrates and biobehavioural correlates. *Philosophical Transactions of the Royal Society*, **359**, 1395–1411.

Dunn, E.W, Aknin, L.B. and Norton, M.I. 2008. Spending money on others promotes happiness. *Science*, **319**(5870), 1687–1688.

Farb, N.A.S., Segal, Z.V., Mayberg, H., *et al.* 2007. Attending to the present: Mindfulness meditation reveals distinct neural modes of self-reflection. *SCAN*, **2**, 313–322.

Gartner Inc. 2020. HR survey on stress levels post-Covid, ARLINGTON, Va., March 19, 2020.

Gillihan, S.J. and Farah, M.J. 2005. Is self-special? A critical review of evidence from experimental psychology and cognitive neuroscience. *Psychological Bulletin*, **131**, 76–97.

Goldstein, J. 2013. *Mindfulness: A Practical Guide for Awakening*. Sounds True.

Goleman, D. 2013. Focus: The Hidden Driver of Excellence, ISBN 0062114867 (ISBN 13: 9780062114860).

Hagmann, P., Cammoun, L., Gigandet, X., *et al.* 2008. Mapping the structural core of human cerebral cortex. *PLoS Biology*, **6**, 1479–1493.

Hanson, R. 2008. Seven facts about the brain that incline the mind to joy. In *Measuring the Immeasurable: The Scientific Case for Spirituality*. Sounds True.

Helen, Y., Weng, A.S., Fox, A.J.S., *et al.* Compassion training alters altruism and neural responses to suffering. *Journal of Psychological Science*, First Published 21 May 2013.

Heller, A.S., van Reekum, C.M., Schaefer, S.M., *et al.* 2013. Sustained striatal activity predicts eudaimonic well-being and cortisol output. *Journal of Psychological Science*, **24**(11), 2191–2200.

Holt-Lunstad, J., Smith, T.B. and Layton, J.B. 2010. Social relationships and mortality risk: a meta-analytic review. *PLoS Medicine*, **7**(7), p.e1000316. doi: 10.1371/journal.pmed.1000316

Kabat-Zinn, J. 2013. *Full Catastrophe Living: Using the Wisdom of Your Body and Mind to Face Stress, Pain and Illness*, Revised Ed. Bantam Books.

Kabat-Zinn, J. 2003. *Mindfulness-based Interventions in Context: Past, Present and Future*. American Psychological Association.

Kabat-Zinn, J. and Davidson, R. (eds.). 2011. *The Mind's Own Physician: A Scientific Dialogue with the Dalai Lama on the Healing Power of Meditation*. New Harbinger Pub.

Killingsworth, M.A. and Gilbert, D.T. 2010. A wandering mind is an unhappy mind. *Science*, **330**(6006), pp. 932.

Laneri, D., Krach, S., Paulus, F.M., *et al.* 2017. Mindfulness meditation regulates anterior insula activity during empathy for social pain. *Human Brain Mapping*, **38**(8), 4034–4046.

Langer, E.J. and Moldoveanu, M. 2000. The construct of mindfulness. *Journal of Social Issues*, **56**(1), 1–9.

Lazar, S., Kerr, C., Wasserman, R., *et al.* 2005. Meditation experience is associated with increased cortical thickness. *Neuroreport*, **16**, 1893–1897.

Lazar, S.W., Kerr, C.E., Wasserman, R.H., *et al.* 2005. Meditation experience is associated with increased cortical thickness. *Neuroreport*, **16**(17), 1893–1897.

Lewis, M.D. and Todd, R.M. 2007. The self-regulating brain: Cortical–subcortical feedback and the development of intelligent action. *Cognitive Development*, **22**, 406–430.

Lieberman, M.D. and Eisenberger, N.I. 2009. Pains and pleasures of social life. *Science*, **323**, 890–891.

Luders, E., Phillips, O.R., Clark, K., Kurth, F., Toga, A.W. and Narr, K.L. 2012. Bridging the hemispheres in meditation: thicker callosal regions and enhanced fractional anisotropy (FA) in long-term practitioners. *Neuroimage*, **61**(1), pp.181–187. doi: 10.1016/j.neuroimage.2012.02.026.

Lutz, A., Greischar, L., Rawlings, N., Ricard, M., and Davidson, R. 2004. Long term meditators self-induce high-amplitude gamma synchrony during mental practice. *PNAS*, **101**, 16369–16373.

Lutz, A., Mcfarlin, D.R., Periman, D.M., Salomons, T.V., and Davidson, R.J. 2013. Altered anterior insula activation during anticipation and experience of painful stimuli in expert meditators. *Neuroimage*, **64**, 538–546.

Lutz, A., Slager, H.A., Dunne, J.D., and Davidson, R.J. 2008. Attention regulation and monitoring in meditation. *Trends in Cognitive Sciences*, **12**, 163–169.

Ong, J.C., Manber, R., Segal, Z., *et al.* 2014. A randomized controlled trial of mindfulness meditation for chronic insomnia. *Sleep*, **37**(9), 1553–1563.

Raub, J.A. 2002. Psycho-physiologic effects of yoga on musculoskeletal and cardiopulmonary function: A literature review. *Journal of Alternative and Complementary Medicine*, **8**(6), 797–812.

Reb, J., Narayanan, J., and Chaturvedi, S. 2014. Leading mindfully: Two studies of the influence of supervisor trait mindfulness on employee well-being and performance. *Mindfulness*, **5**(1), 36–45. Research Collection Lee Kong Chian School Of Business.

Rozin, P. and Royzman, E.B. 2001. Negativity bias, negativity dominance, and contagion. *Personality and Social Psychology Review*, **5**, 296–320.

Seppala, E. 2015, December 14. How meditation benefits CEOs. *The Harvard Business Review*. Retrieved from https://hbr.org/2015/12/how-meditation-benefits-ceos

Singleton, O., Hölzel, B.K., Vangel, M., Brach, N., Carmody, J., and Lazar, S.W. 2014. Change in brainstem gray matter concentration following a mindfulness-based intervention is correlated with improvement in psychological well-being. *Frontiers in Human Neuroscience*, **8**, 33.

Squire, L.R. and Knowlton, B.J. 1995. *Memory, hippocampus, and brain systems.* In *The Cognitive Neurosciences*. Gazzaniga, M.S. (ed.). The MIT Press, pp. 825–837.

Swart, T., Chisholm, K., and Brown, P. 2015. *Neuroscience for Leadership: Harnessing the Brain Gain Advantage (The Neuroscience of Business)*. Palgrave Macmillan.

Takahashi, H., Kato, M., Matsuura, M., Mobbs, D., Suhara, T., and Okubo, Y. 2009. When your gain is my pain and your pain is my gain: Neural correlates of envy and schadenfreude. *Science*, **323**, 937–939.

Tang, Y.-Y., Ma, Y., Wang, J., *et al.* 2007. Short-term meditation training improves attention and self-regulation. *PNAS*, **104**, 17152–17156.

Thompson, E. and Varela, F.J. 2001. Radical embodiment: Neural dynamics and consciousness. *Trends in Cognitive Sciences*, **5**, 418–425.

Uttam, K., Guleria, A., and Khetrapal, C.L. (eds.). 2015. Neuro-cognitive aspects of "OM" sound/syllable perception: A functional neuroimaging study. *Cognition & Emotion*, **29**(3), 432–441.

Walsh, R. and Shapiro, S.L. 2006. The meeting of meditative disciplines and Western psychology: A mutually enriching dialogue. *American Psychologist*, **61**, 227–239.

Reviews of *The Lemurian Revival*

An exquisitely lucid and supremely timely read. Sivadas Raghava's book is an elegant exploration on how Indian philosophies, techniques, and approaches meet the modern era. As the world resides in turbulence, it is easy to get caught in its chaos; and deal with issues that we have not faced before. In that context, Sivadas teaches us to rely on our own deep sense of self, build it, leverage it as a source of vitality. To care for others means starting with caring for oneself, to center oneself and using that as a strength to make meaning of the world. In doing so, Sivadas builds a framework of authenticity and leadership based on modern scientific principles, but is grounded in ancient wisdom. A wonderful book ... I hope everyone reads it.

Raghu Krishnamoorthy
Chicago, USA

Siva's book is a must-read for individuals, leaders, and entrepreneurs, especially in a post-pandemic and uncertain world. He outlines the conscious journey the reader must undertake to spiritually armour themselves in order to become better leaders. The key for any individual to manage professional pressures and overcome them is by building mental resilience and gaining mastery over the self. IQ and EQ are of course important. But Sivadas's emphasis on SQ in his book *The Lemurian Revival* resonated immediately with me. Defined aptly by him as *resilience*, *flexibility*, *compassion*, and *perspective*, he eloquently explores with exemplars how SQ helps individuals bounce back from life's challenges in both their personal and professional lives, setting apart the extraordinary from the rest.

Punctuated with anecdotes, he illustrates to the reader numerous ways to channel their *inner Michael Phelps*, gain spiritual awareness, and swim through the various challenges that professional life presents. With examples of real-life leaders, he demonstrates how one can cultivate a perspective that does not allow existential questions to eclipse one's abilities and talents. Finally, he reminds us that in the constant evolution of the "self," it is the mind that ultimately "matters" and leaders who understand this and cultivate constructive behaviours will resurrect their inner "Lemurians."

Hema Ravichandar
Bangalore

Sivadas sails through building resilience and leadership by beautifully connecting the older tested principles with modern-day context. Inspiring, systematic, and yet captivating. This wonderful and timely book in this pandemic period would spur interest among young entrepreneurs and those who are earnestly trying to be a good leader in the profession whatever they are associated with.

Dr. Kannan Srinivasan
Director
CSIR – Central Salt and Marine Chemicals Research Institute
Council of Scientific and Industrial Research
Gijubhai Badehka Marg
Bhavnagar – 364002, Gujarat, India

www.ingramcontent.com/pod-product-compliance
Ingram Content Group UK Ltd.
Pitfield, Milton Keynes, MK11 3LW, UK
UKHW061541190726
13845UKWH00031B/1150

9 788194 6019